Praise for *The Family Law*

'A writer of great wit and warmth'—KERRYN GOLDSWORTHY,
The Sydney Morning Herald

'Crisply written and outrageously hilarious … Law's black
wit and cheerfully malicious tone make *The Family Law*
an addictive read.'—*The Courier-Mail*

'Very funny … you may find yourself at times almost barking
with laughter.'—LINDA JAIVIN, *The Monthly*

'Benjamin Law's frank, funny, moving and hugely enjoyable
family memoir has launched him as one of this country's
leading humorists – our answer to Law's literary hero,
David Sedaris.'—*The Big Issue*

'Heartwarming … Law is a considerable talent with a long
future ahead of him.'—*Literary Minded*

'Simulatenously weird and instantly recognisable, the Laws
are an Australian family it's well worth getting to know.'
—*The Enthusiast*

'A rollicking series of insights into the life of a pretty awesome
family … for those who love their writing fresh, fun and
packed with laughs, it's perfect.'—*Bookseller + Publisher*

'A vivid, gorgeously garish, Technicolor portrait of a family.
It's impossible not to let oneself go along for the ride and
emerge at the book's end enlightened, touched, thrilling
with laughter.'—MARIEKE HARDY

THE FAMILY LAW

BENJAMIN LAW

Black Inc.

Published by Black Inc.,
an imprint of Schwartz Publishing Pty Ltd
37–39 Langridge Street
Collingwood Vic 3066 Australia
enquiries@blackincbooks.com
www.blackincbooks.com

National Library of Australia Cataloguing-in-Publication entry:

Law, Benjamin, 1982–
The Family Law / Benjamin Law. 3rd edition
9781863957953 (paperback) 9781921825507 (ebook)
Law, Benjamin, 1982–Family–Humor.
Australian wit and humor. Families–Humor.
A828.402

Page design by Thomas Deverall
Typeset by Duncan Blachford
Cover photograph by Ben King

Cover photograph (L–R): Vivian Wei, George Zhao, Fiona Choi, Trystan Go,
Anthony Brandon Wong, Shuang Hu and Karina Lee

Now a major SBS television series produced by Matchbox Pictures

Printed in Australia by Griffin Press. The paper this book is printed
on is certified against the Forest Stewardship Council® Standards.
Griffin Press holds FSC chain of custody certification SGS-
COC-005088. FSC promotes environmentally responsible, socially
beneficial and economically viable management of the world's forests.

FSC
www.fsc.org
MIX
Paper from
responsible sources
FSC® C009448

For my family:
Mum, Dad, Candy, Andrew, Tammy & Michelle.

CONTENTS

The Family Dictionary 1.
Baby Love 9.
The Family Business 21.
Scenes from a Family Christmas 30.
Holes 34.
Tourism 43.
Sleep Cancer 51.
Heat! Vermin! Pestilence! 58.
Tone Deaf 66.
A Room of One's Own 75.
On Nudity 83.
Like a Hole in the Head 91.
Towards Manhood 99.
You've Got a Friend 110.
God Camp 120.
The Pretenders 132.
Skeletons 147.
We Have the Technology 159.
Oceans Apart 167.
Amongst the Living Dead 177.
In the Mood 186.
So, You Are a Homo 197.
Wrecking Ball 210.

*

ACKNOWLEDGEMENTS 219.

He did not consider if or how or why he loved them. They were just love: they were the first evidence he ever had of love, and they would be the last confirmation of love when everything else fell away. —ZADIE SMITH, *On Beauty*

The Family Dictionary

Lately, I've been stitching together a zine for my family that gets passed around over Christmas. It's called *The Family Dictionary*. Designed to resemble a language reference book, it compiles all the new in-house phrases, terminology and punchlines we've developed over the year, alongside helpful illustrations and diagrams. Some entries are universally suggestive and you wouldn't need to be a family member to understand them. No one needs to stretch their imagination to figure out what a *slitoris* might be. *Heurgh* – uttered as if you're dry-retching – denotes disgust and horror at something. *Flahs* is a bouquet of fancy flowers, and *scrongtrum* still sounds funny, even if you haven't seen the difficulty my mother has in pronouncing 'scrotum.' (She's Chinese, and the placing of the 'r' makes it difficult, she says.)

Most entries, though, are more esoteric. Some are hard to explain without the aid of accents. For reasons we've long forgotten, *commence seduction* has to be said mechanically with robot-arm movements; *yeh fookin' pig-nosed slag* – developed during a car-trip competition to find the most crass insult imaginable towards women – has to be Scottish. Other entries demand complex body movements and choreography. The *Pardamonté* is a dance style my sister Michelle has developed, which complements something I do called the *Dance of Despair*. Both resemble rhythmic gymnastics, but instead of using ribbons and clubs in a sports stadium, we use fitted sheets and plastic bags in the living room. It's really something; you should see us in action.

Over the years, though, we've lost too many entries. We were watching home videos of a family trip to London when I rediscovered a backlog of phrases and private jokes I'd forgotten, voices and characters we'd nearly lost. Who could forget Betty, John and Frank, the trio of confused, hearing-impaired seniors who verbally abused each other? And whatever happened to that skit with the incestuous father, where I'd surprise my sisters by violently banging on the bathroom door while they were taking a shower, telling them to let their father in? Oh, the *memories*. My family always joked that my memory was like a sieve, but watching those old videos made me feel as though I had an open drain. Realising I hadn't remembered those moments made me sad and anxious. What else had we lost?

Making *The Family Dictionary* has become an exercise in not forgetting. The zine provides trigger points, reminding me of the childhood fashion parades in 1993, the strange weekends we spent with my dad in 1997, or the family trip we took to Japan in 2008. All of the entries in *The Family Dictionary* have stories behind them, although some are starting to fade.

*

Here's one of them. When our maternal grandmother – my Poh-Poh – died some years ago, my younger sisters Tammy and Michelle and I flew back to Hong Kong with Mum to collect her ashes. Now an orphan, Mum had been devastated by every aspect of her mother's death: how she'd been forced into a cramped Hong Kong nursing home; the clinical way the funeral had been conducted; the impossibility of her joining us in Australia in those final years; the fact she hadn't made it to her mother's bedside in time. Knowing the trip would be depressing, we all tried to buoy the mood by calling the trip the Ashes Tour and making cricket-related jokes.

Once in Hong Kong, the four of us went to a grim, administrative-looking building that could have been a post office. After Mum signed some forms in Chinese script, the staff members fetched the urn from the back room. It was sealed with so much tape that it resembled a parcel from overseas that had been lost in customs and redirected a hundred times over. Mum took it in her hands, looking lost.

'Mum,' I said. 'Are you okay?'

For a moment, I thought she was going to collapse with grief. Instead, she passed the urn to me and fumbled around in her handbag.

'What are you looking for?' Tammy asked.

Michelle looked worried. 'Mum?'

'Take a photo,' she said. 'I want to remember this moment.'

Clearly, my family has a thing for documentation.

The days that followed were punctuated by Mum's spontaneous crying sessions. These were difficult to predict and even harder to help ease. There were variations in the quality of the sobbing, depending on the time of day. In the afternoon, we'd hear sudden gulps of air in our room, thinking it was a broken hotel vacuum cleaner until we realised it was Mum weeping next door. Her crying was gaspy and staccato for her evening shower, completely different from the late-night weeping when she thought we were asleep. In the stark light of day, the weeping would be dignified and silent: single streams of tears trickling underneath dark sunglasses.

At night, after watching Hong Kong television in my hotel room, Tammy, Michelle and I would go back to Mum's room. She'd be propped up in her bed, speaking to her mother's urn as though Poh-Poh were right beside her. We'd watch her talk for a while in secret; then, taking my lead, we'd all walk in, assuming she'd stop. Mum just looked at us and smiled with red eyes.

'Would you like to say something to Poh-Poh too?'

We all took turns, taking the urn in our hands and talking to it as if our grandmother was still alive. It was a little creepy, knowing these were only *some* of Poh-Poh's remains; we knew the rest were held at Tseung Kwan O Chinese Permanent Cemetery in a marble box somewhere. We sat there, trying to start a conversation with the ashes, unsure whether we'd gotten elbows or knuckle, calves or hair.

'So ... Poh-Poh,' I said, scratching the back of my head. 'You okay in there?'

*

By the end of that week, all the crying, tension, urn-talking and relative-visiting had taken us to the edge, and we started to argue. To cheer ourselves up, we ventured to the recently opened Hong Kong Disneyland, figuring that if anything could unite us, it'd be a theme park. But the heightened emotions of the trip had chipped away at our stamina, and the endless array of spinning rides made us nauseous and fragile. By sunset, we wanted to go home. Crowds from every corner of Disneyland converged on the massive castle where the twilight fireworks spectacular was due to begin. After two hours of standing there waiting, cramped and unmoving, we wondered why it was taking so goddamned long.

'This is going to be crap,' I said. 'Does anyone else's legs hurt?'

'Speaking of crap,' Michelle said, rubbing her stomach, 'I *really* need to take a shit.'

'Can't you wait?' Mum scolded. 'We didn't fly all the way to Hong Kong just to miss this. Plus you'll never get back through the crowds this way.'

Michelle bent over a little in pain.

'So, what *is* this show?' Tammy asked, flicking through the pamphlet. 'Is it just fireworks and Disney characters dancing?' She sounded unimpressed.

Mum's face darkened and we knew not to press her. We'd learnt not to overstep the mark. Anything could set her off and it would end in tears. After we had stood there in silence for a while, someone eventually spoke up.

'Wouldn't it be funny,' they asked, 'if Minnie Mouse came out of the castle right now? But instead of smiling and dancing, she just put her hands on her cheeks and screamed to the crowd, "I was *raaaaped*!"'

For some reason, we all doubled up laughing. It wasn't long before we started taking turns scripting out the scenario: Minnie Mouse would come out of the closed doors, her dress shredded, pleading for help, before one of Snow White's seven dwarves dragged her back into the castle and slammed the door shut. The crowd – holding showbags and dressed in Mickey Mouse ears – would hear muffled screams, but would clap softly, thinking it was part of the show. The screaming would continue as the fireworks were lit, exploding all around us, silencing Minnie's pleas for help, while the crowd stood there, baffled and confused. God it felt good to laugh.

'What's *wrong* with us?' I said, wiping tears from my eyes. 'Why are we laughing at this?'

'We're going to hell,' Tammy said. 'It won't be funny any more when one of us actually *is* raped.'

'We probably *deserve* to be raped now,' I said.

'But until that day,' Michelle pointed out, 'we'll be laughing.'

With that, the lights around the park dimmed and all the tourists started whispering and clapping. A booming timpani and brass section made way for a medley of theme songs, and moving images from Disney's vaults were projected onto the castle. Mum grabbed my hand tightly, the way she does when she's overwhelmed and knows she's going to cry.

'You okay?' I asked.

She nodded.

'It's just that Poh-Poh would have liked this,' she said.

The fireworks were beautiful. I never thought I'd be the type to get emotional watching a grown man in a dog suit doe-si-doe with Pluto to the soundtrack of *Fantasia*. And perhaps it was the pent-up emotions of that trip, or because I missed my grandmother, but I started crying a little too.

Since then, the phrases *I was raped!* and *Until that day, we'll be laughing!* have ended up in *The Family Dictionary*. They come up every time we've chuckled at something tasteless and horrible that might one day actually happen to us – having a stillborn child; limb amputation; brain damage; going on life support; being forced into sex. And every time someone says it, I smile to myself, thinking how strange it is that such hideous jokes can remind me of how I miss my grandmother.

*

Right now, I'm putting together the latest edition of *The Family Dictionary*. This year's edition will have ninety-six entries. It's not a universally loved thing. Inevitably, over Christmas, someone is bound to be offended or confused, or feel left out. Sometimes I get the entries wrong. 'It didn't happen that way,' my mother will say, correcting details or giving me facts I couldn't possibly have known. Or Michelle will interject gravely: 'That's not actually what slitoris is.'

'Then what *does* slitoris mean?'

'I'm not entirely sure,' she said. 'But I think it's a fancy word for vagina.' She brightened up. 'Because it's a slit with a clit!'

To most people, *The Family Dictionary* is a collection of stupid and indecipherable phrases, stories that don't make sense. Friends have picked it up, flicked through it, only to say, 'What is *this*?' or 'I don't get it.' Sometimes, it's more pointed: 'Usually you're funny, Ben, but this is just shit.'

When my boyfriend saw the first edition of *The Family Dictionary*, he'd smile or break into laughter when he recognised a joke. Then he'd ask me to explain certain entries. 'What is *three generations of mud*?' he asked. 'Or *wing-toong-boong-tar-len*?'

I'd explain what the entries meant, correcting his pronunciation along the way, adopting the accents, putting on the voices.

'Right,' he said, slowly. 'But some of these …' He didn't have to say it. They were lame and weird, nonsensical and not funny. For a moment, I was offended and we had a small argument. I took *The Family Dictionary* out of his hands, stomped around and closed doors. But a few hours later, to relieve the tension, I broke into a dance wearing a red helmet and suspenders, something that made us both laugh for reasons that don't make sense, and neither of us completely remembers. I'd probably remember if I'd written about it at the time, but it's gone now.

No one else is obsessive-compulsive enough to document all this, so I'm the one responsible for the mistakes I make in putting the thing together. Inevitably, I'll get stuff wrong. There are some things about my family I think I know, some things that are impossible to understand, and some things I don't really get. And every year, when I go to compile *The Family Dictionary*, I'm reminded how flawed my memory is, and how impossible it is to remember things in detail. I know that years from now, we'll pick the dictionary up and come to the conclusion that we were childish and stupid and relied a lot on non-sequiturs and foul jokes for laughs. But until that day, we'll be laughing.

Baby Love

It's a small miracle that more mothers don't kill their children. My mother said that although she'd never experienced post-natal depression, she'd read about it in magazines and instinctively understood where it came from. 'You know, it's those mothers who want to kill their baby,' she said. 'Like that woman from *Blue Lagoon*, the one with the eyebrows. It's natural with all those hormones, I think. Some animals have it too, like those kangaroos that don't want their babies in their pouch anymore. Oh, and that movie about camels, *The Story of the Something-something*. Did you see it? Very touching.'

Still, my siblings and I weren't put off by her negativity. When we were old enough to have children of our own, we discussed our options at the dining table. Were we going to adopt? How many would we have? Would we prefer an older boy or an older girl? Was it okay to have an only child? What would we call them? In the middle of our discussion, Mum snickered from across the kitchen and warned us off the idea. 'Ha, you want to have kids?' she asked in Cantonese. 'Don't even bother. No one should have to have kids. If I had a choice, I wouldn't have had them.'

It was hard not to take this personally. We stared at her, open-mouthed and offended, before mobilising as a unit and howling her down in protest: 'What are you *saying*? You wish we were never *born*?'

She shook her head. 'No, no, you don't get it. I enjoyed motherhood. Having five kids, being a full-time mum, all of that. What I'm talking about is *if I were born now*, as a completely different person. I'd get my degree or career first, then maybe have *two* kids only: no more. Definitely not *five*.'

Tammy, Michelle and I – the three youngest kids – glared at Candy and Andrew hatefully. If history had been rewritten, the three of us would have been the abortions.

To be fair, we also needed to consider what childbirth did to a woman's body. Over the course of twenty years, my mother's body underwent a remarkable and cruel transformation, from a petite, small-waisted Chinese-Malaysian beauty to a pumping, sweating baby machine that spat out five children in quick, bloody, semi-automatic succession. In some mammals, I think, this many children is referred to as a *litter*.

Mum also said childbirth was unbearably, gratuitously painful. When I once asked her to compare and rate each of our births – which was easier, which was faster – she balked. 'No birth is easy!' she exclaimed. 'Of course a *man* would ask that question. Men can't even begin to imagine. Can you imagine squeezing a lemon coming out of your penis-hole? Yes, yes! That's what it's like! I'd like to see a man squeeze lemons out of his penis-hole. OUT OF YOUR PENIS-HOLE, BENJAMIN. You can't even imagine, can you? A whole *lemon* – with the points on each end and everything, except this lemon has *limbs*. Out of your *penis-hole*. PENIS. HOLE.'

She delved into the more graphic details of childbirth for my sisters: how children robbed you of calcium while in the womb and weakened your teeth; how pregnancy made you want to hurl at the slightest smell; how for weeks after giving birth, you walked around uncontrollably leaking blood and milk all over the place, like you'd been shot. I usually had a strong stomach for gore, but her frank descriptions left me feeling light-headed.

'Plus, every woman's vagina *tears* when they have their first child,' she continued. 'With your first-born, you're bound to get stitches.' When she was in labour with Candy, she underwent an induced labour before her doctor said words no woman should ever have to hear. 'Jenny,' he said gravely, holding a syringe to the light, flicking it with his fingers. 'What I'm going to do now is put a needle in your vagina, then I'm going to cut it with a scalpel.'

In retrospect, Mum said, she was glad he sliced her open. Nowadays, she said, some doctors let your vagina split open naturally, insisting it was better than cutting you with a blade and stitching you up. 'No *way*,' Mum told my sisters. 'Letting it tear will make you look like you have third-degree burns down there. My only advice to you is this: If you have children, don't let your vagina tear. Tell your doctor: *stitch*.' Still, she suspected that after five children, none of it really made a difference. 'After that many childbirths, your vagina meat goes all floppy,' she said, wrinkling her nose. 'Not so stretchy. Dingly-dangly.'*

For some women my mother knew, falling pregnant was a difficult business, an exact and fraught science. They needed to synchronise and schedule everything in order to conceive,

---

* A few days after this conversation, my mother phoned me. 'Just in case you write about this,' she said, 'I wasn't referring to my vagina. My vagina is fine. Write that down: my mother's vagina is fine. In fact, my vagina hasn't been touched in so long, it has sealed back up.'

mark their calendar with the rhythms of their menstrual cycle, analyse their partner's sperm count, map out weather changes, ensure the stars were aligned. Then there were women like her, so obscenely fertile you could get them pregnant by raising an eyebrow in their direction or handing them a bouquet of flowers.

Mum had fallen pregnant with Candy almost immediately after losing her virginity – which, for her, coincided with her wedding night.

'Not much fun there,' she said. 'Not much foul play.'

'You mean "foreplay,"' I said.

'What's the difference?'

When I explained it to her, she laughed and shrugged.

'Doesn't sound very different to me,' she said. 'Anyway, I didn't know I was *that* fertile. It runs in the family, though. Look at my mother: seven children. It's our genetics. If you weren't gay, I guarantee you would've gotten some girl pregnant by now. And if your sisters weren't on the pill, they would have gotten pregnant a *long* time ago.'

*

When she was twenty-one and pregnant for the first time, my mother found herself subjected to a suite of ancient superstitions that my father and grandmother had imported from mainland China. Having grown up in cosmopolitan Malaysia and Hong Kong, Mum found them ridiculous, but did her best to play along.

Some of the dietary requirements seemed faintly plausible, like avoiding watermelon or pineapple – which, they believed, were just asking for a miscarriage. But other requirements were curve-balls, like the nine-month enforced ban on attending circuses and barnyards. The belief was that if she was exposed to living animals for too long, her baby could come out covered in hair (contact with apes) or with a snout-like nose (looking at pigs). All of this also explained why Mum didn't have a single photograph of herself pregnant: Dad insisted the flash could make their offspring cross-eyed or blind.

She found childbirth itself even more humiliating. 'The most embarrassing moment in any woman's life,' she told me, 'is when she's giving birth. Crowning, crowning, crowning, and everybody's just looking at your *hole*, waiting for something to pop out, like a prize.' The first time it happened, it was like a strange nightmare, where she found herself in stirrups and watching doctors impale her with what looked like a knitting needle. Warm liquid burst out over her legs and spilled into a pan. Feeling defiled already, Mum got out of the stirrups only to be handed a giant adult nappy. 'Wear this,' a nurse said bluntly. She changed into the nappy and shuffled back towards her hospital bed, exhausted and ashamed, until the nurses started screaming at her in shrill, scandalised voices.

'*No-no-no*, Mrs Law!' they said. 'Don't go back to bed.' They pointed sharply at the door, jabbing with their fingers. 'Walk outside! Up and down, up and down! NOW.'

Like a humiliated pony at a royal show, Mum began to walk slow laps, round and round, while other patients stared at her shamelessly, fascinated by the bloated Asian woman in a diaper parading for them all. But just like they said, the contractions sped up soon after.

The next two pregnancies were blurs. Her body reacted to Andrew's pregnancy – her first boy – in strange new ways. Her pelvis felt split open like a fractured hull and she walked like a double amputee in physiotherapy, shifting her weight between two swollen, artificial pegs. Andrew wasn't any heavier than Candy, but his skeleton seemed longer, and he fought for space with her vital organs. By the end of it, her liver felt bruised, her kidneys misshapen. Giving birth to him felt as though her entire spine were being rearranged.

Still, Andrew's birth was easy compared with what came later. 'A miscarriage,' she explained to me, 'is like someone's switched on a tap of blood that can't be turned off.' Even now, she'll remind people that she was pregnant *six* times, not five. She was admitted into hospital during the day, but woke up from general anaesthetic at night, in a darkened ward full of sleeping women. Although there were no nurses or doctors to confirm what had happened, she knew.

Groggy from anaesthetic and blood loss, she was sent home the next morning; the hospital needed the bed. 'I wasn't even there that long, and then they *discarded* me,' she said, before correcting her English. 'Not "discarded," sorry. *Discharged*.' On the way home, Dad drove while Mum watched the scenery go by: bitumen and rocks, dirt and gravel. It was the start of spring, but everything looked dead to her. Dad didn't know what to say, and Mum was too exhausted to start a conversation. What was there to say? Silently, Mum swore in future to avoid all procedures where she'd be rendered unconscious.

All she needed was some rest and to be treated gently. But when she got home, she was immediately cordoned off and quarantined, like someone with Ebola or swine influenza. Chinese superstition dictated that she be hidden away from the world. Her situation was a bad omen, possibly contagious. So late at night, while my father showered, she huddled up close with her two toddlers and turned on the television. Candy and Andrew gurgled, laughed and screamed as together they watched variety shows. Although three pregnancies had surrounded her with children and noise, my mother couldn't remember a time when she'd felt lonelier.

*

After I was born, my parents reached an exciting turning point in their marriage: they began to fight openly and without reserve, like two cats thrown in a sack and swung around wildly. Why hold back? they figured. Shouting is so much more satisfying! My mother learned to scream; my father screamed back. Every marriage starts with passive aggression, but couples soon realise that being passive requires effort. It's easier to be openly hostile.

On the night I was born, my father drove their new red Ford Cortina, speeding down the newly paved roads that cut straight through to Nambour Hospital. It was night, and the powerful headlights of the new car made easy work of the darkness. In the backseat, Mum was sprawled out without a seatbelt, her legs crooked and raised while she panted like a walrus. Watching the night sky through the rear window, Mum saw streetlights and stars whip past in a quick blur of whites and yellows against the black. When another set of contractions punched into her groin, she groaned.

'Ugh, it's *coming*,' she said. 'It's *coming*.'

Dad quickly turned a corner, applied the brakes and clambered out of the car. At that moment, Mum felt a wave of calm wash over her. *We have arrived at the hospital. Everything will be okay*. Her breathing slowed; her heartbeat resettled. Then, after staring at the quiet evening sky for a while, she began to fret. Why was it so silent? And where had her husband gone? Where were the nurses? Just then, her mother-in-law's head poked through the rear window and hovered above her, like a hallucination.

'*Ah-Jun*,' my grandmother said, still wearing her work apron. 'Are you in pain?'

She connected the dots later: instead of arriving at the hospital, they'd parked at my dad's restaurant. Hungry, he'd sped to work to grab some leftover rice for dinner. The delay meant that by the time they got to hospital, Mum was already crowning. Nurses swarmed around, almost skipping, and cried out to her in sing-song voices. 'Jen-*ny*!' they trilled. 'We won't have time to shave your va-*gi-na*!' As my mother huffed her way through my labour, all she could think about was the various ways she could kill my father.

Their fighting continued and crescendoed right through to 1986, when Mum was pregnant again. When she was due for a standard check-up and scan, Dad stayed in the car while Mum gathered up her belly and walked to the waiting room, tiptoeing on legs tied up like Christmas hams in maternity tights. It was meant to be a quick affair, a thirty-minute check-up at most, but waiting-room dramas turned it into an exercise in tedium that took over an hour. My father was livid.

'Thirty minutes!' he said when she finally emerged, shaking his head and starting the engine. 'You said it would take thirty minutes. Do you even have a concept of what thirty minutes is?'

They drove and argued; argued and drove. When the lights turned red, Mum got out of the car and slammed the door.

To her surprise, Dad called her bluff and sped off when the lights turned green. No U-turn; no pleas to get back in. He was gone, on his way to work. To get home, she would need to navigate a course of pathways, parks and bridges so narrow that passing trucks would create gusts of wind so great they threatened to lift her – a heavily pregnant woman – off her feet. By the time she got home, she was out of breath and ready to give birth. The nurses had been right: walking helped the process a lot.

Some days later, while she was cradling Tammy in hospital, her gynaecologist – the affable and bizarrely named Doctor Dick – sat beside her. 'Jenny, you can count as well as I can,' he said. 'You're thirty-two now, but this baby is number four. Physically, your body's probably had enough. You should think about tying your tubes.' She was nearly won over by the concept, but balked at the idea of going under general anaesthetic again. And because it never occurred to her to ask Dad for a vasectomy, she was pregnant again three years later with Michelle.

After Michelle was born, Mum was too exhausted to open her eyes, but could hear Dad and his mother in the room, murmuring softly to each other. It took a while before she realised that Dad was consoling his mother. But what about? *Had something gone wrong with the baby?*

'*Leui-jae doh hoh*,' Dad was telling his mother in Cantonese. *Girls are fine enough too*. He said this to console my grandmother, who was hoping for a son, but Mum took it personally. After giving birth to five children, she felt like someone had finally come clean and summed up her role in life: that as a woman, she wasn't anything special, just adequate enough. *Leui-jae doh hoh*. By the time she opened her eyes, my father and grandmother had gone, and everything in her line of vision was streaky and blurred. She began to sob, snotty and miserable.

In the end, Mum reluctantly went under and got those tubes tied. She left the hospital feeling numb, and barely acknowledged Dad's presence as he opened the car door for her. As he drove, she looked at her new baby, who slept inside the rented car capsule. Sleeping and quiet, Michelle looked like one of the plastic babies Mum had seen in toy shops, all perfect skin with poked-out lips like she was about to kiss you. When the car hit a bump, Michelle woke up, sleepy-eyed and dough-faced. Mum laughed to herself: she'd almost forgotten how cute babies were. It wasn't much, but it was enough.

*

When all five kids spend time with Mum nowadays, we slip into childhood habits. We take long naps in the day, shop or swim in the afternoon, then gross each other out over the dinner table with stories that involve poo or sanitary pads. Lately, for kicks, we've started a new tradition of showing each other foul videos we've found on the internet. I'd already shown everyone the video with the two girls and the cup, as well as the one with the cyst being popped open. This new one began with a sombre warning: 'This video contains graphic scenes of an elephant birth.'

We all watched with hands over our mouths as a pregnant elephant started pacing in her enclosure, stretching her body, her trunk extended horizontally into a silent scream.

'Aw,' Mum said affectionately, her heart clearly going out to her. 'The poor thing's in pain; look at its mouth all open.'

Then out of nowhere, a gooey and mucus-covered sac started to drop out of the elephant's rear, droopy and slimy, like something had prolapsed.

'What,' Tammy asked, staring, 'is *that*?'

The sac kept on extending and stretching out of the elephant – 'Oh *god*, oh *god*,' Michelle said – before slipping out of the mother in one quick, slithery movement and exploding on the floor like a dropped water balloon. Blood and amniotic fluid went everywhere, and the mother elephant daintily lifted her leg as a waterfall of liquid drained out and onto the ground.

Everyone screamed.

'Oh *gross*!' Candy screamed. 'That's *disgusting*.'

While the rest of us made vomiting noises, Mum nodded in solidarity.

'Do you still want to have children?' she said, feeling vindicated. 'That happened to me *five* times.'

We all looked at her.

'You're not an elephant, Mum.'

She put her palms up, frustrated.

'What-*ever*,' she said, rolling her eyes. Then she started telling us those familiar stories of old Chinese superstitions: how she'd been quarantined after her miscarriage, prevented from petting animals, denied being photographed while pregnant. Back in China, she went on, aggrieved mothers would beat themselves between their legs whenever their children misbehaved, slapping their vaginas and moaning horribly until they bruised themselves. It was an elaborate public display of regret, signalling that they wished they'd never had children.

We stared at her, silent and wincing.

'That,' I said eventually, 'is a hideous story.'

'Why are you telling us this?' Andrew asked.

'Well, I just wanted you to know I've never done that,' she said. 'Never even thought about it, even when you've misbehaved or caused me pain.'

'Right,' I said. 'Well that's reassuring.'

And in so many ways, it was.

The Family Business

In Hollywood, they have these celebrity tours where the general public are guided from mansion to mansion. The point is to ogle. Look: this is where Oscar-winning actress X lives on summer vacation. Over here: a bungalow where Emmy-nominated actor Y was shot dead in 1989. If you're adventurous and fit, you can buy a map and do it by foot – a pair of binoculars around your neck, an autograph book on hand, just in case you're lucky and encounter a celebrity caught out on bin day. Otherwise, you can pay a fee for shuttle buses and buggies to pick you up and zoom you from Affleck to Damon, Spielberg to Streisand.

Similarly, if I picked you up in a car and drove you around the Sunshine Coast, we could make a little tour ourselves, tracing my father's various business ventures from the mid-1970s to the present-day. There's the restaurant in Caloundra where my parents first planted themselves as two dewy-eyed newlyweds just arrived from Hong Kong. Over in Minyama, you'll see a pink and blue Asian supermarket, my father's biggest gamble, where he found out the hard way that most people are still content to cook Asian food from a jar, rather than use the raw ingredients.

Our road trip would be a strange coastal pilgrimage, through bustling Thai restaurants by the sea and sex shops in suburbia, to deserted takeaways near abandoned theme parks. All over the region, we'll find randomly chosen plots of land, marked in Dad's mind for unspecified projects I can't even begin to understand. Present me with a map, though, and I could place coloured thumb-tacks on all the spots where my father has built, opened, developed or invested in something. Link them up, and we've got ourselves a bit of a tangle.

*

All of Dad's businesses can be traced back to 1975, a time when Australians saw China as the epitome of exoticism. China: it was on the other side of the world. You dug through tectonic plates and bulldozed through the centre of the goddamned earth to get there. Tiananmen hadn't happened, so Australians didn't yet associate the place with massacres and bloodshed. What they knew of the Chinese was limited to a few scattered things like communism, and what seemed to be their national cuisine: deep-fried slabs of hacked-up hog meat, slathered in artificial sauce and served with rice.

If you lived in Caloundra, you would have ordered this meal from my parents, two of the first Chinese people to arrive in the area. In contrast to Hong Kong – a throbbing, stinking metropolis of concrete, where people hung out their laundry thirty storeys up – Caloundra was a ghost town. Literally so: everyone was white. On their first day there, unpacking suitcases and moving around boxes, Dad came up to the bedroom to see Mum pushing her hands against the bedroom window, perplexed.

'What's wrong?' he asked in Cantonese.

'Oh nothing,' she said, retracting her hands like she'd been caught out.

'Tell me,' Dad said.

She put on a weak smile. 'It's strange, that's all. This window's sealed shut.'

Dad frowned. 'That can't be right. Here, let me try.'

But no matter how he pushed and shook it, the thing wouldn't open: it was sealed up and airtight. Dad's mother and uncle, who'd moved into the house with them, tried too, but the window wouldn't budge. Soon, they realised everyone's rooms had the same problem. Dad crossed his arms.

'It's no big deal,' he announced. 'Plenty of air coming up through the stairs, right?'

For the next few years, upstairs became an oven of badly ventilated bedrooms. In summer, they kicked off the sheets in their sleep and woke up stewing in sweat. Their restaurant, Sunny Village, was downstairs, where everyone slaved over woks and grills, undergoing a weekly cycle of burnt fingers and broiled faces. There were other problems too, like the army of stray neighbourhood cats, sent moaning and insane with pleasure by the kitchen's meat scraps. When one jumped into the restaurant's kitchen in a single neat pounce, Mum screamed. It hissed at her, took some meat in its mouth and ran off. After Candy was born, Mum put an umbrella over her bassinet, just in case the cat returned with rabies.

After Mum quit work and Dad leased a new takeaway called Sun-See, it was rare to see him during daylight hours; work rendered him almost exclusively nocturnal. In the mornings, when Mum would get us ready for school, he would lie immobile under the blankets, having fallen asleep only three hours earlier. After we'd put on our school uniforms and eaten breakfast, we'd sometimes stand next to the bed and poke him.

'Mmm?' he'd ask in his sleep. 'Mmm?' He continued to snore,

oblivious. When we got back from school, he'd already have left for work.

During the school year, there would be fleeting windows of opportunity for Dad and I to see each other. When I woke up in the middle of the night, sleepily trudging to pee, he'd be in his usual spot: watching television in the living room, eating fruit with a small kitchen knife. Nothing much changed about this routine except for the fruit – kiwis, apples, starfruit – which depended on the season. He'd always be watching an episode of a Cantonese soap opera, one of the stack of videos he trucked between the Sunshine Coast and Brisbane, distributing them to what seemed like the entire region's Chinese community. These melodramas had been recorded from television to video, and then copied from tape to tape and transported from Hong Kong to Macau, Melbourne to Sydney, Brisbane to the Sunshine Coast. By the time they got to Dad's video player, the colours were satu-rated and bleeding, the audio buzzy and sharp. After flushing the toilet, I'd watch them with him, lying on the sofa, dozing in and out of consciousness, trying to follow the latest family scandal.

'What's happening?' I'd ask groggily.

He'd point to the television with his fruit knife. 'See this woman? She had an affair,' he'd explain, 'and now she is crying because both of her men have left her.'

'And what's this other woman saying to her now?'

'She's saying it was all her fault.'

'Wow,' I'd say. 'What a bitch.'

Dad would nod in agreement and pop a bit of chopped apple in my mouth. The next day, I'd wake up in my own bed, not remembering how I got there.

*

By the time Dad was running his new restaurant, Happy Dragon, his reputation had taken off. Situated in a beachside hotel resort, it boasted a cocktail bar and framed art you plugged into the wall. When switched on, the picture simulated a real, flowing waterfall, which blew our minds. In summer, we'd drink pink lemonade and swim in the resort's freezing kidney-shaped pool, pretending we were famous and devastatingly rich, which – to some extent – we were. By then, Dad was earning enough money to send all five kids to a private school, and our pocket money became spontaneous and unplanned, like some demented game-show. Here, have five dollars a week! Or how about twenty dollars to cover the fortnight? Here's fifty dollars today! Dizzy with success, Dad drafted plans to realise a lifelong dream: an Asian supermarket, on top of which we'd live in mansion-like splendour. When he laid out the first blueprints in his study, all five children gathered around, gawking.

'Will we get our own rooms?' we asked.

'Of course!'

'And a rooftop pool?'

'Yeah, a rooftop pool would be awesome!'

Dad laughed. 'Okay! I'll see what my architect can do!'

Everyone kept shooting out ideas: a rec room, a bike rack, a guinea-pig hutch, a spa bath, a rooftop bridge, an enclosed space for the dogs and various barnyard animals we'd buy. On Dad's desk-sized pad of paper, I started sketching what my room would look like, and the exact spots where the powerpoints, fitted lights and chandeliers would be. In all the excitement, none of us noticed Mum's absence. The whole time, she stood by the door silently, outside of the conversation, arms by her side, watching.

*

My parents' separation a year later was devastating: it was really difficult to accept that we weren't going to get that rooftop pool. Dad went ahead with the Asian grocery store anyway, moved upstairs, and we worked there on weekends. As a staff member, I was clumsy. Once, when I was scanning a bottle of dark soy sauce through the register, it slipped from my hands and smashed on the granite bench, exploding in a million shards, black sauce spraying in all directions.

'Oh no,' I said.

When I looked up, a brunette mother in her forties – kids waiting in the car – was covered in the stuff. Her white blouse was stained black, with small white islands of fabric where the soy hadn't touched her. It was in her face and hair, tiny speckles of liquid like dew drops gone foul.

'Oh no,' I said, unable to think of anything else to say. 'Oh no.'

'It's fine.' But she said this motionless, standing there in her badly applied blackface, as though moving might make the situation worse. 'I'm all right.'

Without ceremony, she picked up her groceries and walked towards the car, seemingly in shock. Biting my lip, I watched her leave.

'See you soon!' I called out. 'Please come again!'

Not only was I clumsy, I was a pathological liar. When customers asked me something I didn't know, I suddenly became an oracle on anything Oriental or food-related. The merits of five-spice. The freshness of duck meat. The political situation in China. Could you freeze bean sprouts? Sure you could! Later, I'd find Dad in his office. He'd visibly aged since leaving the restaurant and starting up the supermarket. His hair was getting whiter, and he was losing sleep from accounts that didn't add up.

He'd look up from his paperwork and smile at me. We'd chat for a while, and I'd eventually ask him for cooking advice.

'So, can you put bean sprouts in the freezer and defrost them for later?'

He made a face. 'Of course not. They'd go all slimy like slugs. They have to be eaten fresh. Within *days*.' He rubbed his temples. 'Why?' he said. 'Who asked?'

'Oh,' I said. 'Nobody. Just curious.'

*

It wasn't long before Dad closed the place down and was forced to sell. I felt partly responsible. He couldn't go back to Chinese restaurants. In the years that had passed, they'd become a joke – dinky novelty eateries that displayed Christmas lights in April and served food on mismatched melamine plates. Melamine. Even the name suggested something tragic and poisonous, something that might kill you. The Chinese were being pushed out to make way for other ethnicities. In any other context, this would be called ethnic cleansing; in hospitality, it was just called business.

So Dad became Thai, just like my uncles in Canada had turned Japanese. I'd never seen him work so hard. Tammy and I worked at his Thai restaurant in the holidays, and the shifts were frantic. Dad would work behind the counter, a multi-tentacled blur of efficiency. One moment, he'd be pulling out the emptied guts of rice-cookers; the next, he'd be removing something from the fryer with one hand and garnishing satay sticks with the other. Every night, I came home smelling as if I'd worked all day in a rancid margarine factory. Even after soaking my shirt, it would stink of grease. I'd take extra-long showers to work off the grime, and then I'd look into the mirror and notice bags under my eyes. With a mixture of fascination and horror, I realised I was starting to look and smell just like Dad.

*

All of us want Dad to retire soon. There are only so many times you can see your father sweating in an industrial kitchen while angry mothers scream at him, demanding their takeaway. But none of this has stopped the flow of business projects that keep him awake at night, each scheme more harebrained than the last. Recently he called me out of the blue to look up a website that traded in gold bullion: he'd read in a Chinese newspaper that lacing gold into your tiles and walls would purify the air. When we did our research and discovered that even small amounts of gold would cost hundreds – no, thousands – of dollars, I exercised tough love.

'Dad, you can't believe everything you read in these newspapers,' I said.

It reminded me of when we were kids, and we'd sit with Dad while he read the same Chinese tabloids. In one edition, there was a photograph of a twelve-year-old girl's face, which was somehow attached to a pig's snout. She looked sad. 'What does it say, Dad? What's wrong with her face?' Dad read the story to himself, looking serious and squinting. Then he announced: 'This girl. She is half person, half pig. The newspaper says this is what happens when humans have sex with pigs. Disgusting.' The papers he read weren't exactly the most reputable sources.

'But the scientists said gold is the best thing for your health,' he said now. 'It clears the air.'

'So wear a gold bracelet. Buy a ring.'

'It's about being healthy,' he said.

'You want to purify the air?' I said. 'Go for a jog. Plant a tree.'

Although I was getting impatient, I also felt needlessly bullying.

'Okay-okay-okay,' he said, sensing my frustration. 'We'll talk soon.'

Because I have a writing degree, he'll still hand over crisp new correspondence for me to peruse and decipher: letters from council; quotes from builders; blueprints from architects; flyers about rezoning laws. It's a world I know nothing about. Even though I tell him this, he says he still wants my opinion. For whatever reason, what I think matters to him.

Even now, whenever I'm on the Sunshine Coast, I'll get stopped in shopping centres by perfect strangers, men and women in their fifties and sixties, who ask me whether I'm one of Danny's boys. It's not surprising: our physical resemblance is growing stronger. And when I say yes, they tell me that Danny's like a star around here, and pin me down with stories about the first time they met him in Caloundra, or how they miss the Asian groceries he used to sell, or the meals he made them at Happy Dragon. But what they love most of all is the Thai restaurant he's got right now, which has become a local institution.

But that's only part of the picture, I want to say, and I almost offer to take them on a tour of all his businesses: the ones that took off, and the ones that faded out. It'll end with a stop at his latest project: towering extensions to his old house, which he plans to rent out or sell. If you were to drive past it more than once, you'd see the place expanding like a pop-up book in slow motion. You could watch it sprout balconies and improvised-looking storeys from the original base, like a tree that's begun to sprout new and unlikely branches. It's the home of a star, you'd think, or the place where a local celebrity must live.

Scenes from a Family Christmas

Tree. Growing up, I thought all Christmas trees were hideous, but it was only ours. Our mother always insisted on decorating the 1.5-metre plastic shrub with every school-project decoration we'd ever made. Up went the cardboard Jesuses, cotton-wool sheep and pipe-cleaner shepherds we'd crafted. My friends' Christmas trees were picture-book perfect, while ours was a melted showcase of texta and clag. Eventually, my mother got a new model: it's miniature, electronic and rotates. Now, when I sleep in the living room, its fibre-optic wires illuminate the walls, like I'm in the high-roller room of the P&O *Fairstar*. Now that's class.

Puppy. We were allowed pets, so long as they weren't mammals. Fish: yes. Dogs: no. If they didn't bite, they'd pass on worms; if they didn't maul, they'd stain carpets. They were like children and our mother already had five of those. Still, my Christmas wish-list that year was one word, repeated over and over. PUPPY. When my mother started yelling at me, I wept in protest. 'It's just my dream!' I cried. 'Aren't I allowed to dream?' This continued until I began to adopt the same vocal cadences as Martin Luther King Jr; then I stopped because it was insulting.

Uncle. Over the Christmas holidays, we'd spend time with my grandmother's myriad siblings, elderly people who smelled of camphor. In my father's car, we'd yow-cheh-hoh, a Chinese term that meant driving without a destination. Because the car was always too cramped, we'd take turns sitting on the lap of a man we simply called 'Uncle.' When the car started to move, he'd massage our laps, a little too slowly, a little too gently. Afterwards, we compared notes and protested to our mother. From then on, we insisted, none of us were required to sit on any man's lap, including Santa's.

The Holy Spirit. As a child, I had an aversion to all avian life, having watched Alfred Hitchcock's *The Birds* at too young an age. Then, in my first year at a Lutheran school, I learned about the Trinity: the Father (a creator), Jesus (a man) and the Holy Spirit (a dove). At Christmas, learning about Jesus' conception upset me. He only existed, I discovered, because the Holy Spirit had impregnated Mary without her permission. In my family, we had a word for this, and it started with 'r.' The fact a bird was involved was too awful for words.

Rudolf. As a teenager, I had terrible acne, the type that not only looked disgusting, but physically hurt. My secret wish was that I'd wake up on Christmas Day and suddenly have no pores. (As a bonus, I'd have developed actual eyelids, too.) Anxious and inflamed, I tried a suite of remedies before facing everyone at the Christmas table. Aloe vera; witch hazel; Clearasil. Then, in desperation, I rubbed lemon juice on my swollen nose, which was a mistake. Later that day, Andrew made me cry by singing one carol, over and over. It was about a very special reindeer.

The Space Between Us. At the family counselling session, we'd been asked to draw family members as dots, mapping out the relationships between each other. If the dots were close, the relationship was strong; if the dots were distant, the relationship was cold. It reminded me of the Christmas before, when Mum had insisted on visiting Dad with us. Despite high hopes, it ended in catastrophe: tears and screaming. By the end of it, we all stood there unmoving, hands by our sides and crying, mapping out our own distances from each other, like constellations of stars, some light years apart.

Seafood. It'd been a rough year. Christmas needed to be perfect. Everyone was assigned specific food to prepare, and one sister was responsible for seafood. On Christmas Day, however, there was none on the table. 'We'll just buy it today,' she said. But calls to the fishmongers confirmed they were closed. 'Are you retarded?' I asked. 'Who's open on Christmas Day?' My over-reaction shocked people. Instead, I made lamb, and became emotional when people avoided the gravy. It had been made of blood: the lamb's, of course, but the way I was acting, it may as well have been mine.

Hypotheticals. Over Christmas lunch, we play a game of hypotheticals. 'Would you rather drink a bucket of piss or eat a teaspoon of poo?' Tammy starts. Everyone else weighs it up – urine's sterile, but the shit would be over quickly – but Michelle responds quickly: 'Bucket of piss!' Mum prefers the urine too. 'Shit is so dirty,' she says. Andrew remains silent, so we press him. 'I wouldn't choose either,' he says, which disappoints us. 'What if someone was holding a gun to your head?' I protest. He stares at me. 'Well, I wouldn't get into that situation, would I?'

Long Distance Call. I'd resolved to tell Dad I was gay before the year's end, and Christmas was only a few weeks away. Eventually, I just rang him at work. 'Does your mother know?' he asked. I said that she did. 'What about Candy – does she know too?' Again, the answer was yes. 'And your brother?' At that point, I knew how the rest of this would go, and I regretted having so many siblings. 'It's okay,' he said eventually. But I knew he was referring to the gay thing, not the fact that he was the last to know.

Poverty. There's an unspoken but fierce pride that despite all the odds, and despite all the family history, we still fundamentally like each other. One of the ways we prove this is by purchasing gifts. Over the years, this exercise, especially over Christmas, has become financially crippling. There are just too many siblings. When Candy floated the idea that we do a Secret Santa, everyone balked. But we like gift-buying, we insisted. Now we can't recant. So the cycle continues, and we wallow in extreme poverty throughout January and February, surrounded by shiny gifts, assured that we are loved.

Holes

Australian primary schools are hellmouths of violence and misbehaviour. Over the years, my sister Candy, a teacher, has seen children fight and tear at each other so viciously that they've drawn blood, while other teachers tell me stories about children ripping each other to shreds, teeth and skin flying everywhere. Other kids misbehave in more modest, but no less disturbing ways, like openly masturbating in class with the kind of silent, itchy fervour usually reserved for mosquito bites. If you're a teacher, Candy explained, the most appropriate response is not to call out the student and shame them, but to suggest gently that playing with your genitals is more of a 'home activity,' to be pursued in 'private time.'

During my years in primary school, I learned the hard way that friends would even turn on each other for the sake of a laugh. In Year 2, I'd sometimes leave the morning Christian devotions to rush off and pee. The bathroom closest to us was also the most disgusting, shared by around a hundred of the school's youngest boys. Because of their age, none of them had mastered the art of a steady, aimed stream, so the redbrick dungeon always had a shallow layer of urine stewing on its drainless floors like a murky, sick broth. As you tiptoed in, the soles of your school shoes would get wet, and the heady stink of it all would leave you gagging and wanting to cry. Having just left spiritual devotion that day, hell was on my mind. *Hell was a hot place*, the pastor had told us, *a hot place where the damned burned for all eternity*. Hell might be hot, I thought, but it would also smell like this.

As I unzipped my fly, my friend Andy – a spectacled imp of a kid – came in behind me. With his thick glasses and crazy eyes, Andy was known as a practical joker, which was one of the reasons why we liked each other. We made each other laugh.

'Just wait, Andy,' I said. 'I need to go first.'

Andy put up his palms, as if to say, *That's cool with me.*

'Hey,' he said, as I started to pee. 'Have you seen the trick I do when I pee?'

'What?'

Andy explained how using his stream, he wrote messages, spelled out words, usually his name.

Giggling, I said, 'What? Like this?'

Keen to impress, I started spelling out my name with my stream.

B, E, N, J—

Then, without warning, Andrew pushed me face-first into the trough. Shocked, my hands flew out to stop myself from falling over, and my palms connected with the slick-wet metal, covering my fingers, arms and sleeves in sour wetness. In one quick motion, I slipped back into my trousers but kept peeing, saturating the legs of my pants and socks. Andy covered his mouth, laughing, and bolted.

It was a dirty trick to pull on a friend. Crying and soaked, I asked the sick bay whether I could be taken home by my mother. They agreed, but only after I had changed into a pair of dry trousers eight sizes too large for me, held up by scrunching the waistband together in my hands. I'd like to say my friendship with Andy ended there, but for some reason we continued being friends as though nothing had happened.

On lunch breaks, I'd watch violence take over the school-yard. There was the time my friend Brett's hand was impaled with a freshly sharpened HB pencil, and all the occasions when girls pulled one another's hair out and whipped each other with skipping ropes in vicious lashes. One time, an ambulance carted away a small boy who was bleeding from a cracked skull. Everyone knew that a boy named Guy – a huge, aggressive lout who looked twice his actual age – had hurled a brick at the boy's head. No one had turned him in for fear of retribution. As the ambulance pulled away, Guy watched with his arms crossed and chin pointed upwards, as if to say, *Well, that's the end of that.*

I tried to stay out of trouble. It was only barely tolerable being the victim of a piss-related assault; the idea of being the aggressor or culprit – of marching to the principal's office to explain myself – was unimaginable. By the time I hit Year 3, I'd developed an impenetrable reputation as the most obedient Asian student in the school. With my bum-part hair and straight As, I could do no wrong.

*

That same year, Mum was heavily pregnant with my sister Michelle. Although it was Mum's fifth baby, she kept reminding us that it was her sixth pregnancy; she'd lost a baby the year before I was born, and didn't want any of us to forget. As a result of so many pregnancies, her body was starting to give out. In those final months, she had to wear specially designed beige medical tights on her legs, presumably to prevent them from crumbling beneath her like termite-eaten beams. When I came home from school in the first week back, I found her slouching in bed, propped up with a pillow, rubbing her stomach and unable to move.

'Mum, can you sign this?' I said, passing her a piece of paper.

'What is it?' she asked.

It was a permission slip for Mrs Reed's Year 3 sex education program. Mrs Reed was a woman with sharp features and a slightly nasal British accent. She sounded the way I imagined an aristocratic English cat would sound, if such a thing existed and was able to speak. Signing the form meant Mrs Reed would teach me all about reproduction – stuff I knew already, thanks mostly to Mum's explicit accounts of childbirth and my late-night torch-lit readings of *The Joy of Sex* in Dad's study.

'I'll sign it, but I don't know why they need to teach you this stuff,' Mum said, handing the slip back to me and smiling. 'The other kids, I understand – but you?'

Still, the lessons were surprisingly frank. As a class, we were accustomed to Mrs Reed reading to us from giant storybooks the size of a desk, but we never thought there'd be sex education versions featuring massive, three-dimensional pop-out reproductive organs. Monstrously large-scaled labia opened and folded at us as Mrs Reed turned the pages, like fleshy, winking vertical eyes. *Wink, wink*, the pop-up labia seemed to be saying to us. *Nudge, nudge.*

When Mrs Reed turned the next page, a massive ball-sack stared us in the face, silencing us.

'This,' Mrs Reed said solemnly, 'is a scrotum.'

With her finger, she proceeded to outline the wrinkly sac of skin, which hung out of the book sadly. We got the sense Mrs Reed didn't much care for the scrotum. She gave it a wary look, as if to say, *So, we meet again, scrotum, my old nemesis.*

'And this,' she said, unimpressed and turning the page, 'is a man's erect penis.' The giant cardboard penis popped out, fully aroused, pointing at us like a giant, accusing finger. Involuntarily, we rocked back. As she showed us the different parts – the vas deferens, the urethra, the glans – her finger slowly traced the cardboard shaft of the thing, up and down.

Outside, it began to rain.

'When an adult male is aroused,' Mrs Reed said, 'the body pumps lots of blood into it, so it becomes stiff. Sort of like …' She trailed off.

'Like a ruler?' someone asked.

'Like a bone?'

'Like a sausage after it's been in the freezer?'

'No,' Mrs Reed said. 'It's more like …'

'Like a rock?'

'Like a brick, except shaped like a sausage?'

The bell for lunch-time rang.

'Well, look at that!' Mrs Reed said, snapping the cardboard penis shut, making it retreat immediately. 'Time to eat.'

While the other kids filed out for lunch, several of us chose to stay inside to avoid the downpour. When we were sure no teachers were around, we opened the pop-up book and started to giggle. We made the labia wink again, then turned it sideways to make it talk like a massive cardboard mouth. 'Her-ro!' we made it say. 'My name is Mrs Labia, and my appetite is *gi-normous*! I love eating everything, especially doodles! Pleased to *eat* you!' After we'd endowed every pop-up representation of genitalia with a name and personality – Little Miss Ovaries, Annie the Anus, Clarence the smooth-talking Clitoris – the impersonations of Mrs Reed began.

'Scroo-tum!' I screamed, straightening my spine, putting on a harsh British accent and pointing at the 3-D ball-sack with a sharp metal ruler. My impersonation of Mrs Reed was uncanny and everyone knew it. 'Tes-ticle!' I said, turning the page. 'This,' I said in Mrs Reed's voice, 'is a vah-*jarn*-ah! Show me your vah-*jarn*-ah, girls!' Everyone laughed at my comic genius. Then a girl named Courtney interrupted.

'Ben, no!' she said. 'Look!'

Everyone gasped and saw the same thing: I'd been tearing the book to shreds with the square edge of the metal ruler. Appalled, I stopped breathing, my mouth hanging open. I turned to my friends, only to find they'd run from the classroom, escaping the scene.

When we reconvened in the afternoon, Mrs Reed's face was red-hot with rage. She made us sit on the floor again and perched the book on her lap, flicking through each page, slowly and accusingly. Looking at them was sickening. The pop-out genitals hung out of the book defeated, all pock-marked and savaged; organs, tendons and nerves flopped out at wrong angles, like the wires of a telephone thrown against the wall. The kids who'd gone outside at lunch-time stared at the book open-mouthed. The rest of us looked to the floor.

'When I came back to return the book to the library,' she hissed, 'what did I find? *Holes*.'

Each page she turned made me wince, and my bottom lip began to tremble. 'No one is leaving this room until I have the names of those who damaged this incredibly expensive book,'

Mrs Reed said. 'We could be here all day, unless one of you tells me what happened. I'm more than happy to wait.'

At that moment I understood what a 'heavy' silence meant, how you could actually *feel* the oppressive weight of a room full of people holding dangerous knowledge that could indict you. Something had to give, and when it did, it would hurt like nothing else. Already, I could see what was going to happen, and when it did, none of it surprised me: the snitching in front of the other students; the public declaration of my involvement; my croaky admission; Mrs Reed's shock; the other kids giggling; the tears of humiliation as I handed the book of mutilated genitals back to the library. *What kind of a sick child are you?* the librarian wanted to know. It was all too much for a seven-year-old to bear.

*

By the time Mum gave birth to Michelle, Mrs Reed seemed to have forgotten about the pop-up book incident. The world of education took a new turn, towards promoting self-esteem and 'special-ness.' See Michael in the corner, who can't control his bladder? He's 'unique.' Stacey, over there, who's plagued with warts all over her hands? She's 'interesting.' In this new spirit of promoting everyone's unique qualities, we spent a lesson filling in the blanks on a sheet called 'ALL ABOUT ME,' which we would personalise and then hang on the classroom wall. We filled in our name, our age, our interests. Then we got to a section that said: 'I am special because ...' While everyone else fretted, that section was easy for me.

'A year before you were born,' my mother would tell me, 'I lost my baby. Yes, Mummy miscarried. Oh, I know, it made

Mummy so sad! I was bleeding like someone had *stabbed* me – there was so much blood. Afterwards, all I wanted was to get pregnant again, have another baby in me so I wouldn't go crazy from all the sadness. So soon, Mummy got pregnant again and – like magic! – exactly a year after Mummy lost her baby, you were born! To the day, can you believe it? And that's why you're so special. You're Mummy's miracle baby.' It was a strange story, and burdened me with a weird sense of guilt: the only reason I existed was because another potential sibling had died before I was born. Still, it reminded me why I was special.

But when it came to filling out Mrs Reed's activity sheet, I got confused. I knew 'miscarriage' meant a baby had died before being born, but one girl in my class had told me 'abortion' meant the same thing. *Abortion*: it had a nice modern ring to it, which I preferred. So I began writing: 'I am special … because my Mum once had an abortion. And exactly a year later, she had me.'

To this day, I can only assume Mrs Reed felt a misguided pity for my mother. What else could explain why my activity sheet was hung up with everyone else's? She must have assumed my mother had undergone a horrific, government-sanctioned abortion in China and then – horror upon horror – had me a year later, a child born of hideously bad timing and fortune.

Months after I'd realised my mistake, I would wake up at night, panic-stricken at the memory of broadcasting such an incendiary, untrue story about my mother. At least when bad children were caught, they were punished accordingly. There was opportunity for atonement: scores could be settled, sins forgiven. But no one knew about this, and no one ever would, mainly because I couldn't explain the crime. How could I even begin to explain? *I broke your vase. I took your money. I spilled the milk.* Those are easy to admit. But how does a seven-year-old even begin to say, *I accidentally told my entire class you had an abortion?*

For years, everyone had thought I was such a good boy – so polite, so hard-working – but now the cracks were starting to show. I was the boy who'd vandalised books, the pervert who'd mutilated the reproductive system, the son who said dark, unspeakable things about his mother. At night, I'd sob quietly to myself, knowing I was an impostor, convinced I was nothing but bad news, believing I deserved whatever punishment was coming my way.

Tourism

My family isn't the outdoors type. Despite being raised on the coast, Mum detested visits to the beach (all the sand it brought into the house), while Dad disapproved of wearing thongs ('It splits the toes'). We never camped. All those things involved in camping – pitching a tent; cooking on open fires; the insects; shitting in the woods; sleeping on rocks; getting murdered and raped in the middle of nowhere – they never appealed to us. 'We were never camping people,' Mum says now. 'Your dad never wanted to camp, and insects eat me alive. See, Asians – we're scared of dying. White people, they like to "live life to the full," and "die happy."' She pauses. 'Asians are the opposite.'

We preferred theme parks. For parents raising five children, theme parks made so much sense. They were clean and safe. There were clearly designated activities, and auditory and visual stimuli that transcended racial, language and age barriers. Also, you could buy heaps of useless shit. This is an exercise at which Asians of all backgrounds seem to naturally excel. Venture into my childhood home, and in amongst the epic piles of suburban debris you'll still find a plush blue whale wearing a Sea World cap, T-shirts emblazoned with Kenny and Belinda – the now defunct Dreamworld mascots – and a pox of fridge magnets commemorating each visit.

It was family tradition that once a year, our family of seven (eight, including my grandmother) would cram ourselves into a 1990 grey five-seat automatic Honda. Faces smashed against the glass; no leg room; the two smallest children illegally wedged between various legs – we travelled like this for a good three hours before we reached the Gold Coast. We'd fall asleep at such extreme angles that our spines contorted. When we woke up, our shirts would be covered in drool we weren't even sure was ours. By the time we got to the theme park, our limbs were numb, our nerve endings destroyed.

On the day of the trip, we'd wake up before sunrise in order to get there by opening time. Despite enduring three hours of vivid pain in the car, we'd feel an overwhelming sense of awe as the Thunderbolt, Dreamworld's rollercoaster, painted with flames, emerged from the trees that bordered the Pacific Highway. It would appear so suddenly, like a strange apparition or a mirage. We would crane our necks back, trying to take in the sheer majesty of it. For a non-religious family like ours, the experience was borderline spiritual.

Once through the gates, we kids would do our best to distinguish ourselves from the Asian tourists. We'd make our Australian accents more pronounced and end our sentences with 'eh.' Our trousers were pulled further downwards, away from our navels. We refused to wear bumbags, and spoke English very loudly, with proper grammar and syntax. The hordes of Japanese and Chinese tourists would point to the most innocuous objects and proceed to take photographs like idiots. We could only imagine what they were hollering to each other as they churned through their film. 'Look, a fire hydrant!' 'Over here, a drinking fountain!' 'Wow, there is a toilet: a public, shared facility and receptacle for my waste. Why not take a photo of it!'

Mum would sabotage all our efforts to set ourselves apart. She wore her hair in a Bozo-esque clown perm and insisted on wearing her fluorescent Dreamworld T-shirt if we happened to be at Dreamworld, and her killer-whale Sea World T-shirt if we were visiting Sea World.

'Mum, come on,' I said, as she posed us at the entrance of yet another ride. 'Everyone's going to think we're tourists.'

'We *are* tourists,' she said. 'Now smile big!'

It would take her about twenty seconds to press the shutter. Once the button was finally pressed, it would take another five for her to release it.

*

When my parents split up, I was twelve years old and had just finished primary school. Trips to theme parks became less frequent. Custody was split. Mum hated driving long distances. Dad threw himself into work at the restaurant. The mood became downbeat and glum. The separation also made our family the subject of gossip amongst the local Chinese community, whose members were scandalised. Elderly Chinese women who smelled like mothballs and grease would corner my siblings and me in the shopping centre, pulling us to one side, shaking their heads and clicking their tongues, lecturing us in Cantonese.

'*Wah*, what is going on?' they'd ask, raising their tattooed eyebrows. 'You need to tell your parents they must make an effort to get back together! *Ai-ya*, why would any parents split up like this? You're only children! And no marriage is a walk in the park, is it?'

None of these concerned citizens ever visited my mother during this period. Mum was always a tiny woman, but she began to lose weight quickly and her low blood pressure got worse. She became prone to intense dizzy spells that would immobilise her for days on end. At my fourteenth birthday party, she almost fainted.

Mum and Dad instituted a rotating custody roster. The five schooldays, Monday to Friday, were considered neutral territory; it was the weekend that was considered important family time. Mum and Dad would take turns, Dad taking us for every second weekend. But despite these days being technically 'Dad's,' Mum insisted on coming with us, declaring boldly that it was her right as a mother. Plus, when did *she* get to go to theme parks? Never. And who was she going to go with? *Herself?* It made far more sense for her to come along, she said.

Poor Dad. It really put the pressure on him to make those four days a month memorable and worthwhile. At the time, he was working as a chef in a hotel at night, and sleeping during the day at his mother's place. He couldn't afford the luxury of time, so when it came to his designated weekends, Dad needed quick and convenient options. He needed theme parks.

*

The Sunshine Coast hinterland is a haven for miserable theme parks. In contrast to the Gold Coast's pleasure domes (Dreamworld, Movie World, Sea World), which are show-offy and grand, garish and decadent, theme parks on the Sunshine Coast are poor-cousiny, half-arsed and afterthoughtish. Come to Superbee, where our prime attraction is free honey tasting! Also: you can buy honey! Look, here is a man dressed as a bee! Here at the Hedge Maze, get lost! In a hedge! We also have scones!

On one of Dad's more disastrous weekends, we travelled to suburban Noosa to visit a deserted tourist attraction called the Big Bottle. It was, as its name implied, a giant bottle. You'd climb the staircase inside, which was made up of hundreds of empty beer bottles. Once you were at the top, a giant metal slippery slide curled around the bottle's exterior and you'd slide down on a hessian sack. Inside the bottle, it smelled awful, like the piss of a hundred dehydrated men. Because the entire interior was made of beer bottles, you would never know which ones contained the urine. The bottles weren't exposed to the sun, so the piss never evaporated. It smelled so bad. We never went there again.

Another time, we visited Forest Glen Deer Sanctuary, a typically neglected drive-in wildlife preserve near Yandina. Despite its catchy television jingle, the place was starting to lose business to the reptile park a few kilometres away, which had recently renamed itself Australia Zoo. We bought bags of feed at the entrance, then drove slowly around the dirt track. The deer came up to the car in packs, and we fed them through the windows. Amongst the deer and kangaroo, there was also a single emu. It started walking towards our car, pushing its way past the does and fawns.

'Are we even supposed to feed the emus?' Tammy asked. 'Isn't this stuff just for deer?'

'Maybe it's developed a taste for it,' Dad said.

The emu proceeded to eat all the feed from my hand, then moved on to Michelle's open hand. When we ran out of food, we wanted to keep driving. But then the emu spotted my paper bag, still full of feed and reserved for the deer around the bend. It made a terrible, ungodly noise – an almost carnivorous, honking screech of excitement, not unlike the velociraptors in *Jurassic Park*. Its neck came the whole way into the Honda, and we screamed as pellets flew around the car.

'Drive faster, drive faster!' Michelle screamed.

Dad put his foot on the accelerator and the emu squawked, trying to keep up the pace.

'Wind up the window!' Dad said.

What Dad didn't understand was that because most of the emu's head was in the car already, winding up the window would make the situation worse. But in my stammering panic, I reached out, grabbed the window winder and start winding up. The emu refused to retreat. Its head became stuck, and it croaked and coughed at us, banging its head against the car ceiling in wild, spastic fits.

'Drive slower!' I said, my voice squeaky with panic and puberty. 'We're going to rip its head off!'

Dad slowed down, inching the Honda forwards, but the emu kept up, walking alongside the car, still screeching and honking.

'Stop the car, stop the car!'

We killed the engine, and I slowly wound down the window. The emu gave the car's ceiling one last bang with its head, before sliding its neck out and stumbling away from the car in a daze.

We drove home in silence.

*

A fortnight later, Dad called me at Mum's place.

'So, what's the plan for this weekend?' he asked. 'You got any ideas?'

'I don't know,' I said. 'Haven't we done everything around here already?'

'How about the Ginger Factory? Or Underwater World? You guys like turtles. They're Tammy's favourite, right?'

'We did that last month,' I said, sighing. 'We don't have to go somewhere special every weekend, you know. We could just hang out.'

I detected a faint click over the telephone line and coughed loudly – a clear message to Mum that I knew she was on the other phone, listening in to my conversation with Dad.

'You know, I'm looking to invest in a new restaurant in Pacific Paradise,' Dad said. 'There's a theme park there we should check out. What do you reckon?'

*

Nostalgia Town's motto was 'A Laugh at the Past.' Its main attraction was a family cart-ride, a journey into an era when fibreglass brontosauruses roamed the earth alongside tableaux of Anzac diggers and plastic Aborigines. Slouching, I sat at the back of the ride with Mum, while Dad sat at the front with Tammy and Michelle. In the carts in front of us, mothers and fathers sat alongside each other, their children jammed in between them.

I wondered what they thought of our family, and whether they questioned why the Chinese family's mother and father sat so far away from each other. Maybe it was a cultural thing, they'd think. I'd watch them, wondering how, and why, their parents got along so well. I'd watch them intently: like an outsider, like a tourist.

*

Nowadays, if you drive through Coomera, towards Dreamworld, you'll see the Thunderbolt has been dismantled. Nostalgia

Town has long been torn down, and the deer at Forest Glen have disappeared, presumably having undergone a mysterious transformation into venison. (I don't know what happened to the emu.) That old wildlife sanctuary is now a luxury tourist resort. I can't find any evidence that the Big Bottle still exists, so I can only assume the piss fumes proved a health hazard and that it was torn down too.

Right now, my family's planning to spend New Year's Eve together. Everyone except Dad. We're throwing around some ideas for what to do, since it will be the last time the family will be in the same place, at the same time, for quite a while. Someone has suggested we go camping.

Sleep Cancer

Out of nowhere, my mother developed this thing for buying products from television infomercials. As far as vices of house-bound mothers went, it was better than a valium addiction or having indiscriminate sex with neighbours, so we left her to it. In those rare windows of opportunity when all the housework had been done, the kids were at school and Dad had left for work, what else was there to do?

So Mum would switch on the television, sit in her favourite chair, get herself comfortable with a mug of room-temperature water and acquaint herself with the latest in patented, revolu-tionary inventions: hair-removal devices with hundreds of miniature rotating tweezers; no-name-brand CD players; kitchen appliances with attachable options; bagless vacuum cleaners that could pick up bowling balls. Even now, she regards all of these purchases as necessary, cost-saving devices – except, perhaps, for the body-hair remover. The last time I saw it, it had been hastily unplugged and forcefully lodged in the back of her bathroom cabinet, like it was shoved in there after a sudden bout of fury and disappointment. Upon closer inspection, I found several long, curly hairs lodged in its tiny, angry metal tweezers, like the teeth of a baby shark that had accidentally eaten a wig.

One of the first items Mum bought from the television was a

birthday gift for me: my very first alarm clock. It was a sturdy rectangle of beige plastic, roughly the size of a slim brick, with a cartoon decal of a rooster stuck to the speaker. The rooster was depicted leaning back, puffing out its chest with its beak open, as though making a friendly community announcement. The TV infomercial had shown the alarm emitting a friendly 'cock-a-doodle-doo,' which my mother found adorable and irresistible. *What child wouldn't love this clock?* she'd asked herself. *Who wouldn't love that friendly rooster?*

When we unwrapped the clock and tested the alarm, the resulting noise wasn't friendly at all. It was the sound of night-mares: a horror-movie scream of a chicken having its wings slowly broken and torn off, crying out for its mother. Even though our place was large and made of solid brick, the ringing alarm clock could be heard from the other side of the house, and the tortured pleas of poultry bled into our dreams.

The rooster was only one part of a symphony of noises that made up the morning soundtrack of our home. Andrew would begin by urinating loudly in the hallway toilet, a sound similar to someone pouring a large pitcher of water into a pond. Candy would greet the morning by dry retching as she brushed and flossed her teeth, the result of an abnormally weak gag reflex. Mum would harmonise by clearing her itchy throat with a steady drone that sounded like *Kaaaaaaaah*. As the last one to wake up, my contribution would be the terrible rooster. When I finally silenced it by pressing the 'Off' button, a perky automated voice would chirrup: 'Good morning!'

After my parents separated, I did an audit of all the things in my life that caused me unnecessary stress. This included the rooster alarm clock, which was slowly driving me insane. But because it had been a present from my mother, I knew I wouldn't be able to throw it out; instead, I gave it back to her.

Dad had now left home, and the anxiety and stress of those months saw Mum's sleeping patterns become wild and unpredictable. When she did sleep, it was like a coma – a bear-like hibernation far more insidious and flattening than anything any other family member had ever experienced. Once I had slept for fourteen straight hours when I had chicken-pox, but Mum's sleeping sessions outdid even that. If she wasn't sleeping for most of the day, she would remain awake for hours on end, watching late-night movies on SBS until the after-hours broadcasting signal kicked in, at which point she'd tune in to infomercials for the exercise and julienne machines. It was as if my mother had narcolepsy, insomnia and chronic fatigue syndrome all rolled into one. In the middle of the night, I could hear her, still awake, with the TV murmuring softly in the background. Later, I'd hear her slippered feet skulking around the house, my mother reduced to a tired zombie shuffle.

When school started, the rooster alarm clock once again began releasing its bone-chilling cries into the morning air, but this time from Mum's room. The alarm would continue for minutes on end, and in my sleep I'd wrap a pillow around my head, convincing myself that at any moment Mum would turn it off, which never happened. I always had to march down the hallway to do it for her.

'Good morning!' the rooster said.

In the morning silence, I looked at Mum in the king-sized bed where she now slept by herself. It looked strange without Dad there on his usual side. Because Mum had lost weight since the separation, the bed looked enormous, as though it was threatening to swallow her up. She hadn't budged for the entire time the alarm had been on.

'Mum?' I asked, touching her shoulder. 'Mum? The alarm has been going for ages. Can't you hear it?'

Andrew and Tammy joined me, rubbing their eyes.

'Seriously, someone needs to get rid of that clock,' Andrew said.

Tammy looked at Mum, concerned. 'Is she okay?' she asked.

Mum didn't move as I nudged her shoulder again.

'Mum?'

I leaned over Mum's face to make sure I could hear her breathe. At that moment, to our relief, she opened her mouth and smacked her lips. I put my head close to her, knowing she was about to say something. We all waited in silence for her to speak.

Kaaaaaaaaaaaaaaaaaahhhhhhh.

Some mornings, after switching off her alarm clock, I'd head straight back to bed, tired and grumpy. When one of us would eventually wake up properly, we'd do laps around the house waking up the rest of the siblings, informing them of the emergency at hand.

'All of us slept in!' we'd scream. 'And we've only got eight minutes to get dressed and drive to school! Get the *fuck* up!' It was an awful way to start the morning. Once in the car, we'd pick fights with Mum for the entire trip, all of us desperately knotting neckties and pulling up socks as she sped along the main road, only half-awake, her nerves frayed, still wearing last night's pyjamas.

'Why didn't you wake me up?' she asked. 'You know rushing makes me nervous on the road.'

'You're the *mother,*' I said. 'Isn't it your responsibility?'

'I've been traumatised by a bad marriage! It has affected my health! All the stress has made me very, very tired! Do you know what it's like to be this tired?'

When we reached the school, the final bells would have rung, and I'd file into the worship hall for daily devotion, an unshowered, unkempt mess. Teachers and friends would notice my hair moulded into the form of my mattress, and they'd shake their heads. *Did we know what it was like to be this tired?* Mum had asked.

'Sleep cancer,' my mother said when she picked us up that afternoon. 'I have sleep cancer.'

'What are you talking about?'

'It's like an illness,' she's explained, one hand on the wheel. 'I go to sleep, but when I do, it's so hard to wake up. It's like cancer.'

'You do *not* have cancer,' I said. 'That's a tasteless thing to say.'

'I didn't say I had *cancer*,' she said. 'Sometimes it just feels like I'm dying, that's all.'

*

Having diagnosed herself, Mum went about concocting remedies. Whenever there was illness in the family, Mum's knowledge of Chinese herbs and soups was as important as any prescription a GP might administer. One particular soup would help with her moods and sleeping patterns, but it was complicated: it needed to be simmered for hours, left overnight, then boiled up again in the morning. Since the evening was going to be a television-packed all-nighter anyway, she let the soup simmer while she sat and stared at the screen. That night, reruns of *Family Ties* were playing. A wholesome show about a family that stuck together no matter what, it had long been shunted from day-time schedules. Eventually, she started to lose consciousness, and with her eyes half-open she switched off the lights and shuf-fled off to bed.

We were woken up by alarms we'd never heard before, intense, pulsating flashes of noise that sounded like someone taking an ice-pick to our ears. In my dream, I had been naked, riding down neon-lit waterslides in the middle of the jungle, but now people were telling me to wake the hell up. We were in an underground bunker, and emergency lights were flashing. 'Wake up!' they said. '*Wake up.*'

When I opened my eyes, I saw smoke: the fire alarm had been set off. The first thing I thought was not that we were in danger, but that we were disturbing the neighbours with all this noise. *What will they think?* Sometimes, shame and embarrass-ment are strong enough to override all other emotions. Mum was already in the hallway, using a bath towel to beat the smoke away from her face as she tried to get to the source of the fumes in the kitchen.

'Cover your noses,' she yelled. 'Switch on the fans and open the windows.' The sirens continued to scream into the dark. Coughing, everyone started turning on lights, and we saw there was no fire, but that the herb soup had boiled right down to the base of the pot. The charred remains were smoking and wheez-ing: a black, dried-up mess of herbs. Andrew grabbed two place-mats and waved smoke away from the alarm while Candy opened the windows and turned on the ceiling fans. Tammy and Michelle grabbed onto me as I used my pillow to wave the smoke away.

When the alarm stopped, we stood in a circle, no one saying anything.

'The soup,' Mum eventually said. 'It was the soup for my sleep cancer.'

Everyone looked at the clock on the wall. By its count, the sun would be up soon enough. In a few hours, it would be time for school. We'd have to shake ourselves out of our nightmares, and a rooster would be calling us out of bed.

Heat! Vermin! Pestilence!

In Queensland, the humidity could just about kill you. Unlike in other Australian states, where people talk about experiencing a 'dry heat,' the heat up north is like a steam room, a wet blanket of air that hangs like a drunken fug and smothers your brain. It's what you'd call equatorial weather, the kind of climate where the pores on your face spontaneously open up, and primary schools send pupils home when classrooms transform into furnaces, which is more often than you'd think. All over the state, old men's noses swell up and mutate into red, tumorous cankers from sun exposure, and young boys develop inflamed, peeling shoulders that look like textbook cases of leprosy. You can tell the women who wear sunscreen from the ones who don't. The ones who skip sunscreen have skin like their grandmothers. Their grandmothers don't have skin at all, but a rich, tan, saddle-quality leather draped over their faces.

Where I lived, no one's houses were designed for the heat. Builders and architects were in denial, and our living room gave priority to decoration over ventilation, with heavy ground-to-ceiling windows that didn't open, but magnified the heat before trapping it in like an oven. In summer, you could bake a cake in the ensuite, make pudding in the sinks.

On Christmas school holidays, my siblings and I would lie in front of a rotating fan, rubbing ice cubes on our temples, waiting for the moment the fan's blades would incline in our direction to offer us sweet relief.

'Mum,' the five of us would groan. '*Muuuuum.*'

We didn't even know what we were asking for; the five of us sounded drunk. All we knew was that we wanted the pain to stop. As we moaned, Candy, Andrew and I sprayed ourselves with a dispenser filled with water, while Tammy and Michelle lay down on bed sheets on the floor, wearing nothing but underpants saturated in sweat.

'*Muuuum,*' we'd say.

Mum would come out, sweating and wearing rubber dishwashing gloves covered in suds. She hated when we complained.

'You think *this* is hot?' she'd ask. 'You don't *know* hot. In Malaysia, it'd get so hot you'd want to rip your skin off, but we'd still have to wear a full school uniform. Three layers. *Three.*' She held three gloved fingers up accusingly, all of them moist and dripping. The way she did it made it look vulgar. At her school, she added, there were nuns in full habits who stoically walked through the searing Malaysian heat without ever flinching or complaining. Could we imagine what those nuns' bodies must've looked like at the end of the day – all shrivelled and hot, their boobs poached in their own sweat like half-cooked pork fillets? *Well*? Could we?

There was supposed to be a moral to her story, an answer to her question, but the heat made it difficult for us to concentrate.

'What?' we asked.

Mum shook her head. 'Do something outside,' she said. 'Get out of the house.'

But even she knew that our options were limited. We were afraid of the beach and terrible at swimming. Sometimes we'd have a 'wet day,' where we'd spend hours with the hose on in the garden, pouring bubble-bath liquid onto a plastic slide stretched out over the lawn. Inevitably, someone would get hurt or we'd get into a fight, and one of us would shred our knees or bruise our face. Wet days were strictly an occasional activity. Other times, we'd stand in front of the freezer until Mum told us we were wasting electricity. Most of the time, though, we were content to stay and whinge, which was something we all did really, really well.

*

Though we might have felt deathly, other things thrived in this heat. Mosquitoes, drunk on sweat and blood, would bite us without fear or shame. Sleeping through summer in the room I shared with Andrew, we'd wake up with welts on our feet, palms and face; the next morning, we'd walk around like we'd been shot by rubber bullets.

But the thing I hated the most was the cockroaches, which bred uncontrollably in our kitchen. I didn't have any problem with spiders or silverfish, and mice almost seemed cute. Friends who had snake issues struck me as exciting and adventurous. But cockroaches were the pest for people who lived in dumpsters. There was something shameful about it.

It was our kitchen's fault. Cockroaches loved breeding in and behind the broken, derelict dishwasher, and after we'd turn off the lights, they'd hold revolting orgies underneath the warm coils of the hotplates. The oven had never been installed properly, and there were gaps between the cabinets and the walls where grease built up like a black tarry plaque. We lost cutlery and chopsticks in those gaps. For cockroaches, it was a warm, sticky, disgusting heaven.

At least twice a day, massive cockroaches would crawl out from their corner and into open display in the living room. There was something so outrageously shameless about the way they did this that we'd bay for blood straightaway. Andrew was always the first to launch into action.

'Die!' he'd scream, chasing one with a shoe. The rest of us would jump onto sofas, hopping from foot to foot, pointing and shrieking as Andrew gave chase.

'Kill it! Kill it!' we yelled, watching it zigzag across the living-room floor.

'Where'd it go?'

'Over there! Over there!' we said, pointing to the pile of board games under the coffee table.

'Don't use that,' Candy screamed at Andrew. 'It's my good shoe!'

'Screw your good shoe!'

The cockroach would climb up the wall.

'Over there, over *there*—'

'It's getting *away*!'

Andrew took aim.

'My shooeeee,' Candy moaned.

'I see it!' I said, pointing at the wall.

'Got it,' Andrew said.

Andrew would peg the shoe with startling precision. The initial impact would paralyse the cockroach for a few seconds before Andrew went in for the kill: a series of unforgiving poundings that would reduce it to an unrecognisable mash of guts and legs. The rest of us became bloodthirsty and primal, like in those movies where small-town mobs are taken over by psychotic bloodlust. 'KILL IT!' we'd scream, as Andrew kept smashing the thing into the floor. The bigger ones would explode, their insides squirting in all directions like a splattered boil, with pus and plasma that looked almost human. By the end, Andrew would be bent over and panting, trying to catch his breath, and all of our hearts would be racing, our blood boiling in the tropical heat.

*

Every year, Dad called pest control. Every time he called, we hoped that would be the end of the problem. Somehow, though, the cockroaches always survived. After a pest-control bomb failed to get rid of them for the third time, we reconciled ourselves to the idea of living in a roach-infested hellhole for the rest of our lives. What else could we do? In the summer evenings, when the heat was so intense that it would wake me up, I'd get out of bed to go to the toilet. On my way to the bathroom, I'd casually smash cockroaches with a plastic slipper, before wiping up their remains and flushing them down the toilet. We all did our bit. After one of these bathroom visits, as I made my way to the kitchen to get a glass of water, I thought about the argument I'd overheard my parents having in their bedroom earlier in the day, behind closed doors. It was something that had started to happen more.

As my eyes adjusted to the kitchen's darkness, I could see the walls were moving. When I could finally focus, of course it wasn't the wall that was moving but the clusters of cockroaches that rippled across the kitchen like a nightmarish curtain. When I took a step back, I nearly stepped on one before it crept off into the shadows. As I rinsed my tumbler, I wondered what the point of washing anything was, since everything would be covered in cockroach germs the next morning. *No wonder my parents aren't happy*, I thought to myself. *Whose parents could be happy in this house?* I figured if the pest-control man wasn't going to do his job properly, I'd have to take matters into my own hands.

I'd read in the *Australian Women's Weekly* about a surefire way to trap cockroaches. You got an empty ice-cream container, soaked stale bread in it with fat, sugar and alcohol, and greased the rim with oil. At night, you put the container in the corner of your kitchen and the cockroaches would climb in, driven crazy by the combination of sweetened liquor and grease. They'd try to get out, but the greased sides would keep them inside.

The morning after I made the trap, my siblings and I, dressed in our school uniforms, approached it slowly. The first thing we noticed was a scratching noise from inside. Together, we peered into the container.

'Wow,' one of us said. 'That is so gross.'

Inside was a stack of cockroaches, almost ten centimetres deep, crawling on top of each other. The cockroaches at the base were either dead or drunk, and the living ones were stepping on the bloated corpses of their comrades, trying to escape.

Without saying a word, I carefully balanced the ice-cream container in my hands, while someone else opened the sliding door that led to the yard. In one swift motion, I threw the container up into the air, and it landed upside down on the ground. No one said a thing, but we all knew what to do. As the cockroaches scuttled away – big and small, fast and slow – into the corners of the garden, we screamed and started smashing them into the dirt with our school shoes, hollering like we were possessed. These things had ruined our home, they'd taken over our house, and now they were getting what had been coming to them. Finally, finally, finally, we had the motherfuckers cornered, something to destroy, something we had control over. We stomped and screamed while Mum watched on, bleary-eyed from another evening without sleep.

*

One of the first things my mother did after she separated from my father was to buy herself a new oven and dishwasher. The oven was fitted next to the cabinets without any gaps, and her new stovetop rested magically flat on the bench: no electric coils, just a polished ceramic top that lit red when in use. After the spaces between the bench and the dishwasher were sealed shut, the cockroaches disappeared almost overnight, taking their babies with them. With my father gone, the cockroaches evicted and new household appliances doing her work, my mother seemed to have a new lease on life. When I went to wash my glasses and mugs, she'd holler from the other room, 'Don't worry! I have a dishwasher now! You can use as many glasses as you like!' Then she'd laugh like someone deranged, as though she could barely believe her luck.

Years later, when I was eighteen, I had moved out of home and was living in an old Queenslander, a house that faced south, retained heat in summer and let in the freezing air in winter. In the damp, stormy summers, mushrooms would grow out of the shower fittings and fleas would make their way indoors, even though none of us ever let animals in. When the heat became excruciating, I'd lie in bed all evening with bowls of ice, moaning and nude. I thought I'd escaped them, but this new place was paradise for vermin and pestilence too. Still, I had a system for each species. The mosquitoes would be smoked out. The spiders would be let out gently. The fleas would be fumigated. And the cockroaches would be crushed without mercy, with no hesitation at all.

Tone Deaf

When my dad sees an English word in the newspaper he doesn't understand, he points to it and asks us for the definition. He'll say it a few times to himself, rolling the word in his mouth and chewing on it, until the meaning and the sound collide, soften and stick to his brain like gum. Likewise, when my mum learns a new word from television or conversation, she writes it down in her notebook. If the word is particularly tricky, she asks me to spell and define it, then scrawls it down onto scrap paper and sticky-tapes it to the wall to help her remember its meaning and spelling, the way foreign-language students do in the lead-up to exams. Even now, the word *diarrhoea* is stuck to the dining-room wall.

In this way, every migrant family is the same: children learn from their parents, parents learn from their children. It's all very educational. Controversially, though, Mum insists she first learned the word *cunt* from me. I don't remember the exact circumstances clearly enough to verify the claim, but I wouldn't be surprised if it were true. Mum says that afterwards, as often seems to happen when you've learned a new word or concept, she inexplicably started seeing and hearing it everywhere.

'The next night on SBS,' she told me, 'there was this European movie with a woman screaming at her husband because she found out he was having an affair. She yelled to him: "You only like her because her cunt smells like eggplant!" That's what it said in the subtitles. And suddenly I realised that I knew what this word was. *Cunt.* It was that same word you told me not to use at parent–teacher meetings.' She paused to think. 'I wonder whether I would've worked out its meaning if I hadn't heard it from you. *Smells like eggplant.* Yes. Yes, I think I would have.'

Apparently, I'd given her strict instructions at the time not to use the word amongst friends or even with her gynaecologist. She understood, but has since embarked on a lifelong, covert love affair with the word. The lawn-mowing man who screwed her over? She knows just the word to use. The drunken New Year's revellers who left beer bottles in her yard? There's only one word to describe people like that.

In stark contrast to the dedication of my parents, I've become complacent about Cantonese over the years, to the extent that I'm now uncertain whether I can lay claim to the language at all. Now and then, the same tick-a-box question comes up in forms and surveys, questionnaires and applications, leaving me confused and anxious. 'Do you come from a non-English speaking background?' it asks. 'YES/NO.' It seems like such a straightforward thing to ask, but my pen always wavers. Eventually, I select either 'yes' or 'no' at random. Looking back, I've probably filled out a 50–50 share of 'yeses' and 'nos.' What is your 'language background'? What language do you speak at home? They seem like such simple questions. But they're not.

*

Cantonese is the language predominantly spoken by my parents, and the main language spoken in Hong Kong, Macau and southern parts of China. In and of itself, it's one messed-up dialect.

The audio instructors on my Teach Yourself Colloquial Cantonese CDs are more technical and polite about it, referring to it as a 'tone language.' This means the same syllables, pronounced in different pitches, can mean completely different, incongruous things. Consider this sentence: Goh-goh goh-goh (that older brother there) goh goh (is taller than) goh-goh goh-goh (that other brother over there). Again, that's: Goh-goh goh-goh goh goh goh-goh goh-goh. Pause, then add another goh – with a different tone this time – and you're telling the same brother to cross the road. Depending on how you say it, gau can mean 'dog' or 'nine,' 'enough' or 'rescue.' Mae could mean 'rice' or 'not yet,' 'flavour' or 'tail.'

Because of its tonal quality, linguists describe Cantonese as a language that's sung, which might suggest the language is pretty or melodious. But songs can also be terrible and cruel. Think of the late-night sexual moans of the feral cat, the broken wail of the American coyote, or the screeching of the rabies-infested bat. To my ears, Cantonese is not a sung language at all, but a screamed one, a dialect for bickering, exclaiming over scandals and haggling over meat prices.

But hey: who am I to say? My parents speak Cantonese to me, and while I understand most of what they're saying, I'm basically mute when it comes to speaking the language myself. To outsiders, that seems like an odd arrangement, but the analogy I use is music. Everyone understands the language of music, has an innate comprehension of how it works, but not everyone can play it. When it comes to Cantonese, I can understand the music, but I can't replicate it. Cantonese might be a tonal language, but over the years I've become tone deaf.

*

Of the five siblings, Michelle and I are the worst. When friends see our mother talking to Michelle and me in Cantonese, they say how lucky we are to have a secret language, to be able to talk about people right in front of them without their knowing. When Candy, Andrew or Tammy speak in Cantonese, pointing out the girth of someone's arse or the fact that they've tucked their dress into their underwear, Michelle and I will understand and laugh with them. But when we try to speak, we lose words and grimace into space, silently moving our lips as if we've suffered a terrible stroke. 'Goh-goh … man,' we'll say, pointing to someone behind his back, 'hae-hoe … obese.'

For my twenty-first birthday, my boyfriend, Scott, enrolled me in a short course in Cantonese. It would have been difficult to find. While Mandarin is the language of mainland China – the future gatekeeper of 21st-century economics, the Sleeping Giant, the Slumbering Dragon, the Sneaky Chinaman – Cantonese is considered the obscure and irrelevant poor cousin. The only people this Cantonese language course catered for were the children of Hong Kong migrants whose guilt was starting to play heavily on them, or whose grandparents were dying.

The lessons took place every week at 8.30 a.m. on the top level of an ugly, brown-brick, labyrinthine building that smelled as musty as a disused cellar. It was situated on the periphery of a university campus, in a spot that seemed to be bathed in perpetual shadow. On the first morning, I arrived to meet a small group of seven, all of us smiling nervously at one another as we waited for the teacher to arrive. Nearly everyone there was like me: Chinese kids raised in Australia, trying to regain the language they'd lost. *You are my people*, I thought to myself, privately exhilarated that there were others in the world who shared my inadequacies. I could bond with them.

There were exceptions, though. Peter was the lone white person, an older gentleman who'd recently begun a romantic relationship with a woman from Macau.

'Right now,' Peter told me, 'she speaks no English besides "yes" or "no." And I don't speak any Cantonese at all, so that's why I'm here: trying to reach some middle ground, so we've at least got some basic communication going on.'

Their situation baffled me.

'So how have the two of you communicated up until this point?' I asked.

'Well,' he said, 'I guess you could say we communicate with our bodies.'

I avoided Peter after that.

Two other students also stood apart: a young Eurasian brother-and-sister duo. Between them, they'd inherited the high Oriental cheekbones of their Chinese mother and the regal Norse forehead and nose of their Scandinavian father. The combination made them obscenely, enviably beautiful. Their hands were manicured; they didn't have pores. Looking at them made you feel as though you were bearing witness to the next stage of human evolution, a stage to which you hadn't been invited.

When they weren't studying linguistics (him) or working full-time for an international public-relations firm (her), they modelled for television and magazine advertisements. ('It's more like a hobby,' one of them told me.) Their international names, Sebastian and Claudia, broadcast loud and clear: *We might have been born in Hong Kong, but our parents knew how to name us properly.* Their parents had somehow avoided the Chinese tendency to give their kids jumbled, improvised English names like Daffy and Virgyna, Nester and Cornelium. They could understand Cantonese already – as well as Spanish, French and Norwegian – but had enrolled in the Cantonese class to get a proper grasp of the dialect's structure. Or, as Sebastian described it, 'the architecture of the thing.' I hated him immediately.

Our teacher, Linda, was a Hong Kong-born woman in her late forties, the same age and background as my mother. As a result, I felt acute, personal shame every time I let her down in class, which was often. At our first lesson, she asked us to introduce ourselves in whatever Cantonese we already had in our arsenal. Sebastian volunteered first, and told us not only his name and the undergraduate degree he was studying, but also about an upcoming holiday in which he'd be flying to Norway to meet his 'very good friend.' It was clear to me that Sebastian meant a boyfriend – a boyfriend who, I imagined, modelled for Versace when he wasn't working as a foreign diplomat or training for the Winter Olympics.

When it was my turn, I introduced myself and my Chinese name. *'Ngau-goh joong-mun-mehng hae* … Yuk Nung?' I said. My tones were all over the place. The statement came off sounding like a question.

'*Yuk Nung?*' my teacher asked, peering over her glasses.

'*Hae,*' I said. 'My name's spelt "yuk," like when you're disgusted by something, but it actually rhymes with "book."' Linda pursed her lips. I realised I'd been speaking in English when she'd specifically asked us to speak in Cantonese. *'And I am twenty-one years old,'* I added in Cantonese, sheepishly. Then in English: 'That's all.'

'*Yuk*,' Sebastian said, repeating my Chinese name. '*Yuk?*' He pulled out a pocket translator. He punched in some buttons, and then passed it to Linda. 'Is this the right Chinese character set?' he asked. Almost miraculously, he'd conjured up the character for the first part of my name, the only Chinese script I recognised apart from numbers. Then he said the same character in Mandarin, to make sure he was correct. Linda clasped her hands together in delight. My shoulders slumped.

As the weeks went on, the verbal and spoken assignments got harder. They reminded me of high-school drama examinations, in which poorly performing students had to be prompted for every line before being failed in front of the class. Some students became flustered and clumsy under the pressure.

'*Lae-seurng* ...' Linda prompted.

'*Lae-seurng* ...' repeated the student, a nervously smiling teenager who was the only person worse than me. 'Um, what's the next bit?

'*Mm-seurng* ...'

'*Mm-seurng* ...'

The student paused again, biting her lip. She looked towards the rest of us frantically.

'Uhm, line?'

Because the classes were so early, I'd sometimes catch myself falling asleep at the desk.

'Benjamin?' Linda said. When she didn't get a response, she switched to Cantonese and sounded chillingly like my mother. '*Yuk Nung. Are you awake? Why are you so sleepy all the time?*' At that, everyone started laughing at me. Sebastian glanced over with cool pity. When I realised my eye was crusted over with sleep, I rubbed; the sleep fell onto the desk in clumps. *Ngan-see,*

I thought vaguely to myself. That's what 'sleep' is called in Cantonese: eye shit. At least I knew that.

*

Weeks after the course finished, an advertisement for McDonald's came on the television, featuring Sebastian licking a soft-serve ice-cream cone. 'Oh my god,' I said. I called Scott over from the other room. 'Scott! Scott! This is the Eurasian guy I was talking about. You're going to cream yourself over him.'

Scott came over. 'I resent that,' he said, before turning his attention to the TV.

'That's him,' I said, 'the Eurasian dude from the class; that douche-bag I was telling you about.'

It hurt to look at him. Part of me liked to think that because we shared some racial heritage, I might look like Sebastian from some angles. However, watching the advertisement, I realised that this would require major facial reconstructive surgery. Here was a person who was a better version of me in every single way, and a self-destructive impulse made me want to gauge Scott's reaction to him. I watched Scott closely after the advertisement finished.

'Oh, Ben, he's not that great-looking,' he said. 'In fact, I think his face is sort of weird and girlish.' And just then, with sharp clarity, the Cantonese words for 'I love you' darted into my mind. *Ngoh ngoi lae.*

*

I'm trying to become more disciplined, but my Cantonese is still a joke. Michelle takes the joke further and makes up new

Cantonese words, creating an indigenous dialect known only to my family. When it's Chinese New Year, my dad and grandma will issue the mandatory New Year's greetings Sun-Leen-Fai-Lok and Goong-Hae-Fut-Choi, and Michelle will respond with Choot-Cheen-Yut-Ding, a popular brand of instant noodles from Hong Kong. I admire that. She takes Cantonese tones and bastardises them. If your Cantonese is beyond a joke, you may as well get to the punchline first. It might seem insulting to make a mockery of an entire language, but we only do it because the language has been mocking us for years.

A full semester of Cantonese classes had no discernible impact on my vocabulary. Before I left, having failed our final oral assignment, I stole the library's entire collection of Cantonese language CDs and burned them onto my computer. A single volume usually cost hundreds of dollars, but now I have language lessons whenever I need them.

When I drive long distances – say, to my mother's place – I start the CD lessons from the beginning, saying the phrases over and over until they stick. When I park the car and ring the doorbell, I try to drop the phrases into conversation before I forget them. *'Excuse me, Miss, but Mister Leung is currently busy,'* I say. *'Would you like me to show you to his office?'* Mum pretends to be confused, but she knows exactly what I've been doing.

There are other times, though – like right now – when I forget the word for 'office' altogether. At times like these I find myself staring at a blank wall, wishing someone had stuck a note there to remind me how to pronounce it, and what it means.

A Room of One's Own

Our mother always told us that *hate* was too strong a word. In our household, you could sometimes get away with *bitch*, *slut* and the occasional *fuck*, but *hate* was completely off-limits. 'You don't hate your brother,' Mum would say, correcting me. 'That's such a strong word. You might dislike him very much, but you definitely don't hate him. How could you? He's your brother.' Hearing this, I wanted to ask her what emotion, if not hate, had once compelled her to scream in guttural, animal rage before throwing a frying pan at Andrew with such force that it left her bent over and heaving.

The problem was, when it came to Andrew and me, *hate* didn't even begin to describe it. Andrew, three years older than me, was the sibling who'd once crept up behind me in the kitchen and pinioned my arms before flashing out a large knife – the giant one usually reserved for bones and root vegetables – and whispering in my ear, 'Don't struggle, Ben, just stay still.' With that, he ran the blade across the soft fleshy underside of my forearm, the part used for suicide. When I finally found my voice, I emitted high-pitched wails, like a scandalised eunuch. Then Andrew slapped me on the back of my head and laughed. 'Dickhead, it's just the *back* of the knife!' he scoffed, before showing me my unmarked arm. By the time my sisters arrived to find out who'd died, I'd collapsed on the floor, shaking, holding my arm to stop the imaginary blood loss.

Another of Andrew's favourite pastimes was to pin my arms down with his legs, cover my mouth with his hand and tickle me while I spasmed underneath him in pain, crying silently. My gulping, fish-like convulsions reminded me of an incident in a telemovie we'd seen. Set in an all-women's prison, it followed a new blonde inmate who had been wrongly convicted of murder. On her first day inside, the Bambi-eyed prisoner was cornered by butch lesbians, who massaged their knuckles before pinning her down and covering her mouth. The blonde prisoner's eyes widened in horror, but there was no way to scream: she was well and truly muffled. My siblings and I had watched what followed, covering our eyes with cushions and screaming for her as she squirmed and kicked. *So*, I'd think as Andrew held me down and tickled my sides, *this is what it's like to be raped*.

'Oh, don't be so dramatic,' Mum would say later in the kitchen. 'He only does that because he loves you.' But we all knew Andrew was dangerous. After all, he had worked his way through the siblings, almost methodically, and permanently scarred each one of us. Candy had a pockmark on her face where Andrew had gleefully ripped off a pus-filled chicken-pox welt, Tammy's arm was missing a patch of skin because of a biking accident, and I sported a perfect triangle of missing flesh on my ankle, from the time Andrew had dragged me along the road on my tricycle, attached to his big-wheel with an occy strap. When Michelle was born, my sisters and I conspired to protect our infant sibling from the same fate, but we knew we couldn't do much. The best we could hope for was that she wouldn't lose something she really needed – an eye, say, or an adult molar.

*

It was perverse that out of all the siblings, Andrew and I were forced to shared a room. I never understood why boys and girls were automatically housed together. Andrew and I might have both been male, but of the five children, we were the least alike. Andrew was sporty, and won tennis and karate tournaments; I couldn't throw a ball. While I adorned my side of the room with a giant plush-animal collection, Andrew blu-tacked his walls with photos of big-titted bitches. Andrew towered over his classmates, while I was the weedy kid who had to crawl on his hands and knees to board the bus.

We couldn't fit bunk beds in our room, so Andrew constantly rearranged our two single beds to create the illusion of space. One month our beds would shoulder each other in an L-shape; the next, Andrew would push them side by side, separating them with a long, sausage-like cushion we all referred to as the *dai goo-goo*, which translates as 'large penis.' All this constant moving and rearranging, all this desperate shuffling back and forth: it was the behaviour of captive animals in tight confines.

The only space Andrew properly staked out as his own was the corner where his fish-tank stood. It was a glass case the size of a small fruit crate, sitting on a waist-high wooden stand. Although I wasn't allowed to touch it, I secretly loved this underwater world my brother had made, populated by golden fantails, red-capped whities and bug-eyed blackmoors, all docile and friendly. Once every month, Andrew would change the water, an all-day task that involved hauling alternating buckets of dirty and clean water between our room and the laundry. Old newspapers and catalogues would be layered over the carpet in case of spills. As I watched him measure out the chemicals, test the water's temperature with his hand and care-fully lay out the gravel, I could see that this was something like an act of love.

*

Despite our differences, Andrew and I did share one thing in common. We were both perverts. Every week, we'd scan the television guide to see if there was a listing for the movie *Hot Chili*, a sordid 1985 tits-and-arse comedy that Channel 7 would play every few months. It was the precursor to all those modern male teen flicks, except that it had no discernible narrative: some teenagers go to Mexico; they take off their clothes; they have sex with Swedish dominatrixes. The main drawcard was that it showed nipples.

While everyone was asleep and we waited for *Hot Chili* to start, television commercials came on for dating services and phone-sex lines, soft-focus shots of women in red garters and white lingerie: all the stuff that boys aged nine to twelve love.

Then, over a black screen and the soundtrack of squealing strings, a voiceover informed us that over two horrific nights, Australian television would never be the same again. 'In a small American town,' it sneered, 'an unspeakable evil is preying on the children.' Slow-motion shots showed a storm brewing over an American neighbourhood. A small boy in a yellow raincoat ran along the kerbside, playing with a paper boat in the gutter, until the boat got sucked down a stormwater drain. Waiting in the drain was – of all things – a red-haired clown. Something about that was utterly chilling, and I covered my eyes and whim-pered. For a moment, the thought entered my mind that some images were so scary, they could actually send you insane.

Sounds of thunder were intercut with the kid screaming and the clown laughing.

'Dude,' Andrew whispered. 'I think that clown just ripped the kid's arms off.'

The voiceover taunted us. 'Find out with the rest of Australia, what is … *It*?'

Andrew punched the air.

'We're watching that.'

'No, we're not,' I said.

'Yes, we are.' And though I continued to protest, I knew by the tone of his voice that no matter what I did, he'd win out.

On the weekend *It* was scheduled to broadcast, we were sent to our cousins' place for an extended sleepover. Their household was more strict than ours in most ways – get anything less than an A at school, and you were flogged – but it was more liberal in others. It was rumoured that somewhere in the house was bona-fide pornography on VHS: not like *Hot Chili* where you just saw boobs, but the proper stuff, where you saw a man's *doodle* go inside a woman's *pippi*. They were also allowed to keep pet dogs and watch things that were utterly unacceptable in our household, such as Bruce Willis action movies and gory horror flicks about piranhas.

When night fell, we huddled upstairs with blankets and lay on our stomachs in front of the television. 'Guys, I don't know,' I said. 'Maybe we shouldn't be watching this.' But now the mob mentality had taken over, and we were in too deep. 'Ben,' Andrew said. 'It's about *clowns*.'

Everyone laughed, and I shut up. The first scene of *It* was probably the scariest. 'We all float down here, Georgie,' the clown, Pennywise, told the little boy in the stormwater drain.

Watching that scene, I thought my nine-year-old brain was undergoing a stroke; I'd never seen anything so unimaginably awful. The only redeeming thing about the film was Jonathan Brandis, the handsome blond kid from *The Neverending Story II*, who set out to avenge his little brother's death.

Everything else was terrifying: Pennywise coming out of the school shower's drains; Pennywise appearing between spinning lines of white linen; Pennywise appearing as the moon. This clown was inescapable. Scared to the point of tears, my cousins and I went to the toilet in pairs and kept the bathroom door slightly ajar as we peed. Because Pennywise also came alive in photographs, the next day I secretly took the TV guide bearing his image, tore it into shreds and pushed it deep into the garbage.

For months afterwards, I couldn't sleep. If I did pass out, it was against my will. In my dreams, I would be stalked by shadows of laughing clowns in badly lit sewers, before being knocked over, my arms pinned, my mouth covered, unable to scream. Even during the day, I'd feel faint if I saw an image of a clown with red hair. Family visits to McDonald's became harrowing. I even started wetting the bed, and found myself changing the sheets in the middle of the night. Andrew would always wake up, no matter how quiet I was.

'Ben,' he'd say. 'Again?'

'Sorry.'

Without any lights on, we could only hear each other's voices.

'Ben, it's just a clown,' he'd tell me. But even as he said it, I could hear the hint of an apology in his voice. Then, as I tried to go back to sleep, I'd be paralysed by the idea that Andrew was asleep already, since Pennywise only came for you when you were alone. But then Andrew would cough, and I'd cough a little too, and he'd cough back again, just to let me know he was still awake.

*

It wasn't until I was sixteen that I got my own room. Andrew left home and started living with Dad, one side-effect of our parents' divorce that I actually appreciated. Andrew's bed was shifted out, and to fill up the empty space Dad bought me a massive desk from an office supplies store. This desk was clearly designed for an executive or CEO. The sheer bulk of it made it impossible to change the configuration of my room anymore, even if I wanted to. My nightmares and bed-wetting had stopped, but during those first few nights alone without Andrew, I dreamt of evil clowns smothering me while I slept. When I woke, my heart would thump as though I'd been chased for an hour. I'd turn on the lampshade and catch my breath, staring at the spot where Andrew's fish-tank used to be.

Now that I've moved out of home, the only time I see my old room is when I go back to the Sunshine Coast to visit my mum. When no one else is visiting with me, I'll sleep where my old bed used to be. Old blu-tack stains mark the walls, and there are pockmarks where old adhesives have ripped off the paint. What was once a white wall is now the colour of old teeth. To my adult eyes, the room is unbelievably small, a box just over three metres square. It seems impossible that two people could ever have shared this space. My current apartment's kitchen is bigger than the room Andrew and I shared. Our single beds must have been like prison mattresses to have fit. No wonder we loathed each other: putting two growing boys in these confines was like putting two dogs in a ring.

For a recent birthday, Andrew gave me something unexpected. It was a fish-tank, complete with a proper filter, gravel and chemicals. All I needed to do was choose the fish. The pet-shop owner told me to get all females: it wasn't healthy for two males to live together in such a small space, he said. They'd kill each other. But weirdly, the two fish I've got now are males, and have endured for years, content to swim alongside each other, even though they're completely different species.

On Nudity

Most Chinese people are uncomfortable with nudity. They're not like the Koreans or Japanese, so comfortable in their bodies that they create communal bathhouses to bathe alongside one another, happily chatting the day away as they exfoliate dead skin cells from their breasts and arses. Even white people fare better than the Chinese. In primary school, I was shocked to learn that nudity wasn't an issue for some of my schoolfriends, who had even visited the local nudist beach in Noosa with their families.

'Really, it's no big deal,' they'd say. 'It's what everyone looks like underneath, you know?'

But as they'd casually recount their nude weekends playing French cricket by the seashore, all I could do was summon up graphic images: their mother's leathery breasts trembling while bowling; their father's testicles slapping his thighs like a violent pendulum as he ran from wicket to wicket. Then I'd try not to flinch as I had a small, private revelation: 'Oh my god,' I'd think. 'You have seen your sister's vagina.'

My siblings and I were the kids who used a complicated system of towels and hands-free shimmying to change after compulsory swimming lessons. We loathed school change-rooms. Showering and changing alongside our friends felt wrong, and it felt even more wrong in the company of our teacher, Mr Johnson.

'Dude,' my friend James whispered to me after swim class. 'Check out Mr Johnson's dick.' Both of us turned discreetly, to be faced with a monstrous, veiny rope of meat hanging between Mr Johnson's legs. It was enormous. Like a baby barnyard animal facing its bullish senior, my own penis probably shrunk a little that day from fear. Eventually, I would just leave my soggy togs on after swim class and let them seep into my school trousers for the rest of the afternoon.

The last time any of my siblings saw one another naked was when we bathed together as kids. However, there have been occasional instances – horrible instances – where this unspoken boundary has been transgressed. Most notably, Michelle once accidentally saw Andrew get out of the shower. She told Tammy and me the story one day while we were driving along the highway.

Tammy raised her eyebrows at her, then made a gagging noise.

'Piss off,' Michelle said. 'It was an accident.'

'Oh, Michelle, that's foul,' I said. 'When did you even get the opportunity?'

'Don't look at me like that. I was only, like, twelve or something. It was at his old place, and I didn't realise you could see into the bathroom from—'

'Someone please stop this conversation,' Tammy said, 'before she starts describing what it looked like.'

'What, his penis you mean?'

'Michelle, I said *stop*!'

'To be honest, it kind of looked like a long, hissing sna—'

We cut Michelle off by screaming violently. Though we were driving safely in a car, we may as well have been on a rollercoaster, or being repeatedly stabbed in the abdomen. These were blood-curdling screams. The very idea that Andrew even had a penis was too much to bear.

'Michelle!' Tammy said.

'My ears!' I said.

'Your ears?' Michelle said. 'What about my eyes? They were the ones that saw it!'

She was right. Nodding solemnly, we touched Michelle's shoulder in a gesture of comfort and solidarity. 'Touché,' we said. 'Touché.'

*

Recently, my family and I found ourselves in Japan. We hadn't travelled together like that for over a decade, because there were some basic incompatibilities, such as pacing. Because of Andrew's spidery, stilt-like legs, he always walked ten paces in front of the rest of us and became impatient when we lost sight of him. Some of us interpreted this as Andrew not liking our company, though others insisted it was a disability that came with being so tall. Meanwhile, Mum would shuffle along like a sloth, but one that was armed with a digital camera. Her movements were naturally glacial anyway, but documenting everything she saw in a new environment slowed her down even further. By the end of the trip, she'd used nearly ten gigabytes in memory sticks in as many days.

We'd all made a pact to behave ourselves while visiting Tammy, who was living in Tokyo. As our travel guide, she had told us there were two seemingly contradictory things we'd be obliged to do once there: (1) buy clothes; and (2) get naked. *Onsen* are the country's traditional baths, where mineral-rich warm water is pumped from springs into a series of shared plunge-pools. Men and women are separated into their own sections, but everyone there is unflinchingly nude. Back at the hotel, we discussed visiting the baths as a family. Considering Andrew carried a bottle of instant hand sanitiser everywhere, it was perhaps inevitable that he would refuse outright.

'No way I'm going to bathe where some guy's diseased arse-flaps have just been,' he said, flicking through the hotel's TV channels. 'What if someone's just taken a dump in the water? Has anyone thought about that?'

'Are you sure you can't wear togs?' Candy asked. 'Why do you have to be naked, anyway?'

'Because it's a bath,' Tammy said.

'*Ew*, gross. A bath with other people? No thanks.'

'It's no big deal,' Tammy said. 'Seriously, I've already done it. It's just a lot of old women, and no one looks at you.'

'Don't their tits hang down to their ankles?' Candy asked.

'But it'd be like if you went to Paris and didn't see the Eiffel Tower,' Michelle said. 'Or didn't eat snails, right? It's the cultural experience, or whatever.'

For my part, I vocally championed the idea of going to the onsen. How often did you get to see real-life naked Japanese people outside of internet pornography? Still, part of me had reservations, and they were mainly to do with my hairless body (which resembled a prepubescent girl's), the childhood scars on my legs, and those memories of my Year 4 teacher's penis.

In all of these discussions, Mum had been curiously quiet. 'What about you?' I asked her. 'Would you go?'

We were keen to hear her thoughts. In Japan, Mum had proved herself to be thrillingly unpredictable when it came to personal boundaries. *Entering a Japanese sex-shop selling bestiality pornography?* Yes. *Going on a theme-park ride designed for Japanese children?* No. Mum was sitting on a bed reviewing the digital photos she'd taken that day. She looked pensive and conflicted.

'Well, we saw Mount Fuji, and ate a lot of sushi,' she said, slowly. 'So no: I don't think I need to get naked with strangers to prove I've done Japan.' She shrugged. 'Anyway: why would I need to go? I know what an old pussy looks like. Why do I need to see Japanese ones?' It was decided, then. It would be just the three of us.

*

Tammy, Michelle and I caught the Yamanote Line, then a shuttle bus to a nearby onsen. Mum also came along for the ride, insisting there would be plenty to see without her having to get naked and wet.

'I'll just go shopping,' she said.

'It's an onsen,' I said. 'Not a shopping centre.'

'Then I'll sleep.'

'Where?'

'I'll just find somewhere,' she said, shrugging. 'You know me: I can sleep anywhere.'

On the bus ride over, Michelle intermittently buried her face in Tammy's shoulder and groaned like a little kid, something she does when she's nervous or about to be ill.

'It's going to be *weeeeird*,' Michelle said. 'You're not allowed to look at my vagina, okay?'

'How are you going to avoid that?' I asked. 'You'll be *naked*.'

'Maybe we can just bomb-dive into the water,' Tammy said. 'One hand over our pussies, the other one over our boobs.'

87

Michelle's face brightened. 'Oh, I *like* that idea.'

At the onsen, we were given a few things: a small towel – big enough to cover your genitals – and a locker key.

'Are you sure you don't want to come?' I asked Mum.

'I'm going to the gift shop.'

When she had walked away, I turned to my sisters.

'I don't think there is a gift shop,' I said.

'Neither do we.'

After my sisters and I parted company to strip down in our respective change rooms, I started to fret. Undressing in a locker room is one thing; remaining naked and strolling around is another. There were other concerns, like the possibility of developing an unsightly erection. Not because I'd be aroused, but because it'd be like switching from briefs to boxers: I was afraid my penis would be confused and curious, like a provoked earthworm after its soil has been disturbed.

But after only twenty minutes of scrubbing my naked body next to male strangers, the whole onsen experience became a distinctly un-erotic affair. It was the weekend, and elderly men were taking a break from their retirement homes. Young white-collar dads had their toddlers with them, and loud gangs of naked thirteen-year-olds strutted up and down, joking with each other. After an hour or so, it seemed completely normal to be watching Japanese variety shows, sitting in a sauna hot enough to stew my face, surrounded by wet, flaccid penises.

Besides being deeply relaxing, visiting the onsen affirmed some universal truths for me, such as *Without our clothes, everyone looks the same underneath*, and *All penises look like space aliens*. These men were skinnier than me, fatter than me, hairier than me, uglier than me. Some penises were well manicured and finger-like; others were woolly, stumpy and had so much fore-skin they resembled deflated party balloons. But no one cared. It turned out that my Chinese body blended right in alongside the Japanese ones. It was comfortable. Homely, even.

Later, after we'd stewed for hours, my sisters and I reconvened in the onsen's reception, looking for Mum. She had fallen asleep, sprawled shamelessly on a bench with her mouth open, one hand clutching her handbag, the other holding her digital camera.

'Mum?' I said, nudging her. 'Mum? We're back. You've fallen asleep.'

'You should have just come in with us if you were going to fall asleep,' Tammy said.

Mum sleepily smacked her lips, then, disorientated, made a clicking motion with her fingers: 'Take a photo of me.'

On the ride back to the hotel, Mum slept a little more. I asked Michelle and Tammy whether it had been weird, seeing one another nude. Naturally, it had turned out to be a shame-free bonding experience. Tammy said that at one point, Michelle had been bent over a particularly hot onsen tub, her hands grasping the edge, reluctant to get in.

'Michelle, your *udders*!' Tammy had said. 'Get them away or shield them!'

When they'd started laughing uncontrollably, elderly Japanese women silently arched single eyebrows in their direction.

'We basically have the same body,' Tammy said. 'Except Michelle's tits are bigger.'

In response, Michelle put her hands on her hips, leaned back like a Western sheriff and spoke in a Texan accent. 'And Tammy has a *narrrrce* cunt.'

At that point, I was glad Andrew hadn't joined me. Because as pro-nudity as I'd become that day, I don't think I could have brought myself to compliment his genitals. As a family, we still had some boundaries.

Like a Hole in the Head

The summer my friends and I turned fifteen, we started getting casual jobs. Some of us already had gigs laid out for us, like my friend Brooke, whose family operated an independent ice-cream company. Every weekend, she'd man the stall attached to her family's house, where a cartoon cow told passers-by that their ice cream was 'udderly delicious.' There was something about the cow and slogan I instinctively found gross, though I could never explain what. Maybe it was how the cow's udders stood out: erect and firm. They looked aroused; I think that was the problem.

Other friends worked in retail or hospitality, in franchised businesses that don't exist anymore in Queensland, like Copperart and Franklin's. A lot of them ended up working at McDonald's. These were the guys who'd come to school with work stories that made me gag, like how they dared each other to drink concentrated Coke syrup, or held deep-fried apple-pie eating competitions on their lunch breaks. Because I grew up around restaurants, I couldn't think of anything more foul than hanging around deep fryers and grease all day.

After taking my limited resumé around, I got a job doing night-fill at Big W, the giant department store across the road from my house that stocked everything from sodastreams to industrial-sized bags of horse shit. It wasn't difficult work: night-fill was a fancy word for moving stuff around, pulling stock from the back of the shelves to the front. At night, we'd line up outside the enormous metal doors at the back of the store, all wearing the same navy polo shirts, warming our hands like dockies on the wharves. We'd insert our time codes and clock on, before being led to our departments for the evening.

'Cassie, Jessica and Zoe: you're all in manchester with Kerry,' our supervisors called out. 'Brendan, Chris and Rick: you guys are in petcare with Susan. Benjamin, Sally and Ryan: you guys have home improvement with Mark.'

Mark was a stout man in his forties who had worked at Big W all his life. In those first few weeks, he'd hover over me as I stacked rows of 100-watt light bulbs side by side.

'No *no!*' he said. 'You're doing it *wrong*. You don't do *right-to-left, out-to-in*. It's the other way around. You have to work *methodically*, Benjamin. *Methodically.*' He rolled the word in his mouth like someone who'd just discovered it. '*Methodically*,' he said again, squatting down to demonstrate the art of moving light bulbs. 'Left to right, in to out.'

After a few weeks of this, I swapped my position for the more glamorous checkouts and excelled straightaway. I counted change quickly, mastered the computer system in minutes and made sure all the notes in my till faced the same way. After a few weeks, I was scanning and punching in item codes so quickly that I crashed the entire system: a flurry of quick-moving fingers followed by a violent, satisfying thump on the 'SUBTOTAL' key. Instead of getting the subtotal, all I got was a giant mechanical squeal that rang out through the store. Everyone else's systems shut down with mine, and they started ringing their help bells, raising their hands for our supervisor. I like to think she was impressed by my efficiency.

Chinese relatives I hardly knew came and visited me at the checkouts, drawn to my aisle for my speed. I'd power through queues of customers in minutes.

'Oh, your boy is so fast at those machines,' they'd tell my dad when they ran into him. 'Have you seen him work at those machines? Zoom-zoom-zoom. Your son is like a robot!'

He'd beam with pride. It was such a small thing, but the fact that his son was hard working and speedy was a good sign. Clean-cut, polite, friendly and efficient: clearly, his son was destined for great things.

*

Because we all had jobs, our parents assumed we were disciplined and motivated. The truth was, we were saving money towards new and exciting ways of mutilating our bodies. All my Big W co-workers had pierced labrets or lips, and I started flirting with the idea of getting a tattoo: a barcode on my lower back or upper arm, something edgy to symbolise that I was a misunderstood cog in the machine of society, a number that didn't mean anything to anyone. I backpedalled after I saw someone else at Kawana Shopping World with exactly the same thing, an overweight plumber who'd had a barcode tattooed on his arm. It turned me off the whole idea. The point of being branded with a barcode was to stand out as an individual, after all. Or something.

All the girls I knew were going out on covert missions to get their navels skewered without their parents knowing. Afterwards, they would buy cheap midriffs and parade along the beach, revealing their newly pierced stomachs: angry red welts of flesh healing over a metal hoop, framed by a powdery crust of weeping, yellowish plasma. Others would get their tongues done, a form of piercing which was discreet enough to hide at school.

'Why would you pierce your tongue if people can't see it?' I asked.

'Guys say it really feels good when you're ... *you know*,' they'd say. They'd ball their hands into fists, motioning towards their mouths, then jab their tongues against their inner cheeks. They'd raise their eyebrows as if to ask, *Do you get it? Do you get it?*

'Yes,' I said. 'I get it.'

While girls did their stomachs and tongues, boys did their eyebrows. This was during that brief period when eyebrow rings weren't just for council workers, ageing homosexuals and football players, but a trend that had spread into the general community. Everyone knew there were risks involved, but risks were part of the appeal. We'd heard of guys getting their eyebrow pierced, only for the entire left-hand side of their face to collapse like an undercooked cake. That seemed awesome.

At Big W, older male co-workers with names like Josh and Jackson started coming to work with bandaids on their faces, since exposed piercings were against our dress code. To get around this, they pretended they had head wounds that wouldn't heal. In time, the bandaids themselves became a fashion statement, a mysterious and sexually suggestive accessory: everyone knew what was under there, but all you could see was a large, protruding bulge.

'Wow,' I said to Josh during our lunch breaks together. 'Can I touch it?' He'd peel back the bandaid, and I'd run my finger over the hoop in his face, more slowly than was absolutely necessary. I was close enough to smell his Decoré-lathered hair and

Norsca-infused armpits. Right there and then, I knew that what I wanted more than anything else was a hole in my head. All I needed was the money, and to move out of home.

*

Once I was living in the city, my friends surprised me with a gift voucher for a place that not only sold bongs in the shape of skulls and mermaids, but also pierced every body part imaginable. My piercer's name was Mick. He had a five o'clock shadow and was covered in tattoos, but didn't have a single piercing himself. When I pointed this out, he laughed.

'Well, none that you can see, mate.'

Mick told me he'd grown up in Logan, a shire an hour or so outside of Brisbane, which people took as shorthand for boredom, suburbia and youth suicide. As he disinfected his equipment, Mick told me there wasn't much entertainment out in Logan for young people, so when he was a teenager, he and his friends killed time by piercing each other with sewing needles. They'd start with earlobes and cartilage, before moving on to other body parts: noses and lips, that sort of thing. Later, he lived with a nurse who taught him about anatomy: where the nerves were, how to avoid infections, which bits of the body could and couldn't be punctured. Armed with this knowledge, Mick had built an impressive portfolio of piercings. Anuses were his specialty at the moment, although they required a lot of disinfection, care and the use of hand-mirrors.

'Right,' I said.

'But the most sensitive place to get it done,' Mick said, swabbing my face with alcohol, 'is your Achilles tendon.' He pointed to a photo on the wall, showing a young man's foot.

Shot from the side, it showed the soft corner between the ankle and heel, impaled and studded in a line. Seeing this, I squirmed. 'I *know*, man,' Mick said. 'That's a normal reaction. There are a lot of nerves back there, and you can't run fast afterwards. Otherwise you'll *tear* that ankle apart like a perforated sheet of paper. You know what *perforated* means?'

I nodded.

It didn't take very long. Mick clamped my eyebrow with a stainless-steel device that resembled an oversized eyelash curler and flattened my eyebrow down like a waffle. He shoved a small metal rod through my flesh, leaving a single line of blood trickling down my face. He caught this with a sterilised tissue.

'Got it,' he said, as he fed a brown metal hoop through my brow, before squeezing it shut with a pair of pliers. 'Check it out.' He held up a mirror. My face looked pale and sweaty, and my eyebrow was smothered in a layer of fresh blood. All things considered, I thought I looked pretty good.

*

On that first semester break, I took the train back to the Sunshine Coast to work at one of my dad's new restaurants. When my mum opened the door, she flinched a little before putting her hand to her mouth. She peered at the ring on my face with the intensity of an entomologist. Eventually, she reached over and touched it lightly, then shuddered. She couldn't believe what she was seeing, and asked me whether it hurt. I shook my head.

'So, has your father seen this yet?' she asked.

'No.'

She laughed darkly to herself. 'Well, I'd like to hear what he thinks.'

When Dad came and picked me up for the night-time shift, I opened the passenger door of his Honda and hopped inside. It had been weeks since we'd seen each other and he was beaming. When he saw the eyebrow ring, the smile on his face evaporated instantly.

'That,' he said, 'had better be fake.'

He leaned across to give the ring a tug, then recoiled. He rubbed his finger on his shirt, as if he had touched something rotten and was anxious to remove the smell. When he looked at me again, he made a sound I'd never heard before: a cross between a sigh and a grunt.

'Why would you put a hole in your *face*?' he said. 'It looks like you've been in jail for dealing drugs.' He sat back and assessed me, shaking his head. 'Or a pig,' he said finally. 'You look like a pig. Or maybe a cow. An ugly cow.'

'Cows get their *noses* pierced,' I said quietly, rubbing my eyebrow. 'Not their eyebrows.'

The rest of the car ride was silent; my dad stewed in fury while I scowled out the window, slouching and picking at my eyebrow ring. Dad kept shaking his head, a Tourettish tic his body seemingly couldn't control.

You just don't get me, man, I thought, hooping the ring through my eyebrow, over and over again. *No one understands me at all.*

'Stop playing with it!' Dad said. 'You're going to give yourself an infection.'

There was no way of knowing then, as we drove on towards the restaurant, exactly how mad he was.

*

A few days later, I had a call from Tammy.

'*Sam-Gor*,' she said, calling me by my proper family title.

'Dad's pretty angry. He said to tell you that if you don't take the ring out of your eye, he'll have to disown you as his son.'

'It's my *eyebrow*,' I said. 'Not my *eye*.'

'Whatever. He just said he wants it out.'

It wasn't long before I removed the eyebrow ring altogether, not so much for my father's sake, but because it was starting to smell. After taking the hoop out one evening, when I tried to put it back the next morning the piercing had already closed, as though it had never been meant to be there.

But at that moment, as I finished speaking to Tammy and hung up the phone, I was irate that such a simple thing could come between us. If a metal ring was enough to make him this angry, how would he react when I told him I was gay, or that I had a boyfriend, or that I was studying for a university degree with the word 'creative' in its title, which offered no discernible job prospects? What would happen *then*? The only thing I knew was that once we got to the restaurant, I'd have to work really, really hard to win him back. To have a hole in my face was one thing; to be unemployable and lazy was a shame beyond imagining.

Towards Manhood

There are some men in the world who are unambiguously male. Unquestionably, identifiably, inherently male. It's not uncommon for teenagers I encounter on public transport to be twice my size, and twice as physically developed, even though I'm twice their age. These creatures – who apparently share the same XY chromosome pairing as me – are tall and broad-shouldered. They have feet the size of concrete slabs, five o'clock shadows, legs like carved tree trunks, and they sport hair on their chests and arses. One assumes their genitals swing between their legs like anvils, and their shit stinks like the wet earth. They are, undeniably, men.

When it came to me, it was as though my mother's uterus had had several moments of hesitation in deciding what it'd produce. After coming up with Andrew, my giant of a brother, then having to endure the horrors of a miscarriage, Mum's womb was exhausted and indecisive throughout 1982. 'Well, the baby should definitely have a penis,' the uterus thought. 'Yes: a penis. Slap one on. Should we put hair on its forearms? Maybe hold back on the forearm hair, I don't know. What about leg hair? Yes: leg hair. Actually, no: stop the leg hair. Oh no, wait: *put it back*.'

The result of this indecisiveness was me: an Asian hybrid man-child ... thing. Someone with a 27-inch waistline, hands like a well-manicured woman, unsightly and improvised leg-hair growth, and – inexplicably – a baritone voice that can sometimes sound like a gay James Earl Jones with a cold. Despite my skinny frame and Asiatic eyes, I also have sensual full-bodied lips, not unlike those of a female African-American blues singer.

For most of my life, I've worked against the outcome of this genetic lottery. I've tried bashing shit, listening to different music, gaining weight, building muscle, slouching, pretending to like girls – but nothing's really worked. Now, at the age of twenty-five, I've given up trying. Yes, I'll swear like a stevedore, but I refuse to heckle; I'll belch in public, but will refrain from farting; I grow hair on my abdomen, but not on my calves; I'll eat your meat pie, but not your vagina. I'm a compromised failure of a man.

*

My siblings are fond of reminding me that the signs were there from the start. There's one family video we sometimes bring out at Christmas that shows my four siblings and me, between the ages of two (Michelle) and fifteen (Candy), holding a fashion parade through the living room. My mother never got rid of clothes back then. Pantyhose, old bathrobes, hideous socks with ruined elastic – she kept them all. They went into a massive plastic tub, and voilà: Jenny's Bucket-of-Fun was ready. As a mother of five, she needed cheap entertainment.

A lot of the home video is just screaming and shrieking. At one point, Candy – dressed like a transvestite from a medieval fete – approaches the camera and crosses her eyes. 'I'm a lesbian!' she declares. Delighted, six-year-old Tammy screams with laughter and starts calling after her: 'Darling! Darling! Darling!'

Andrew and I refuse to be outdone. We know we can be more entertaining than a medieval dyke in rainbow glasses. We find old, saggy brown pantyhose and pull them tight over our genitals, past our navels and into our armpits. We strut down a makeshift catwalk made of sofa cushions and head-rests, hands on our arses, blowing kisses to the camera. Tammy laughs, scandalised and confused. Two-year-old Michelle, not really understanding what is going on, screams and screams and screams.

Things get out of hand and Andrew cruelly tries pulling off my shorts, laughing as I stumble over the cushions, still in panty-hose and high-heels. Siblings start running into each other like idiots. Costume changes behind the sliding doors become more violent and frenzied. Dad, who works hideously long nights at the restaurant, comes into the scene, looking disoriented.

'Darling, darling!' Tammy screams at Dad.

'I'm a lars-bian!' Candy says.

Weirdly, the video shows me dry-humping the cushioned catwalk and moaning, pretending I'm a woman orgasming. 'Urgh, urgh, urgh!' I grunt. It is chaos. Then Andrew comes bursting out of the doors and—

Ugh!

—the video cuts to black.

When we return, Andrew is on the floor, bent over and howling in pain. Someone has kicked him in the balls. Actually, from what we gather watching the video, it mightn't have been a kick, but a punch. Apparently, Tammy had balled her fists, aimed, and – without reason – hammered them straight into his testicles.

Andrew crouches, keeled over, crying his guts out.

Behind the camera, Mum sighs. 'Michelle, give your brother a tissue.'

Andrew continues crying, and Michelle waddles over and gives him a Kleenex. It's a touching moment. The mood has definitely shifted from unhinged madness, and we've sobered up. But watching the video now, I know that without a doubt, sitting somewhere out of frame, my ten-year-old self is happily oblivious, still wearing his dress and pantyhose, examining his nails in the sunlight.

*

Around the time of the fashion parade, I'd been having a successful run in childhood gymnastics, and was featured in the newspaper several times for my sporting prowess. After a while, though, the bars started hurting my hands. The exercises became excruciating: 180-degree, full-circle rotations on the high bar called 'giants'; supporting my entire body weight in a 90-degree L-shape on the rings; spinning my legs around a pommel the size of a shetland pony. I was entering that painful transition period when male gymnastics becomes less about nimbleness and agility, and more about brute strength and courage. Lacking both of those qualities, I quit. People told me it was a girly pursuit anyway.

Andrew recruited me into the decidedly more manly sport he was pursuing: karate. None of this cartwheel, leg-splitting bull shit. Now I was moving on to a sport that involved bashing the living shit out of people, which was as manly as it got. During one of my first lessons, our sensei – a white dude called Eddie – told us how in shopping centres, he always kept an eye out for potential attackers by watching his reflection in glass store entrances and window displays. He always kept his hands balled in fists, just in case.

'You just *never* know,' Eddie told us. 'One of the main ways people get attacked is from behind. They never see what's coming. Sure, you might call those attackers "cowards." You might say they're not even *men*. But calling them names won't make any difference when they've slit your throat and you've got blood all over your shirt. Newsflash, kids. You are now *dead*. No more pulse. Your parents are calling the cemetery to make funeral arrangements.

'So do what I do: watch for people in reflective surfaces. Stay alert. And when those bastards attack, be ready to smash their faces in.' He punched the air in front of him. 'Like *this*!' Everyone nodded sagely.

Eddie's presence made karate a more frightening prospect than it had to be. Even though I was fond of the *kata* routines, which seemed more like a choreographed dance than martial arts, I showed no aptitude for karate's actual bashing component. My gymnastics training gave me the flexibility to kick a fully grown man in the head, but there was no strength behind those blows. My frail little boy-bones meant that you could have probably broken my collarbone by tapping me on the shoulder. The freestyle sparring sessions were the worst. 'Green-belt,' a stout orange-belted girl said to me one night, beckoning me with her finger. 'You're with me.' One well-aimed kick to the gut later I was winded.

Even though Andrew and I walked to and from karate class together every week, I'm not convinced we bonded during that period. We were just too different. He was the boy of the family: a monosyllabic, grunting champion tennis player who smelled weird and punched holes in walls to vent his frustration. I was on the primary-school debating team, jumped skipping ropes during recess and had a defence mechanism that involved a combination of scratching and spitting.

'What *are* you?' Andrew asked one night, withdrawing from a fight after I had repeatedly spat in his face and clawed at his eyes, squealing like a pig. He wiped away the soup of saliva and phlegm that marinated his face, and looked at me with utter disgust.

'I mean, really, Ben: what *are* you? Fight back properly. Be a man.'

Our musical tastes were irreconcilable. It was 1993, and Nirvana had just released *In Utero*. Andrew would listen to the fourth track, 'Rape Me,' over and over again. He didn't have a personal stereo, so Kurt Cobain's ironic plea for someone to sexually abuse him droned from the living room into everyone's bedrooms and the kitchen where Mum was cooking dinner. Apparently, it was what guys listened to, but even as an eleven-year-old I thought the song was pretentious and embarrassing. Why would anyone want to rape Kurt Cobain? He was greasy, married to Courtney Love, wore flannel and clearly did not look after himself.

Instead, I immersed myself in another seminal album that was released the same year: Mariah Carey's *Music Box*, a serious and studied meditation on love ('Dreamlover'), bravery ('Hero'), loyalty ('Any Time You Need a Friend') and profound loss ('Without You'). I ordered it from the back of a *TV Week* catalogue, along with Bryan Adams's *So Far So Good* and Billy Joel's *River of Dreams*. I would listen to *Music Box* endlessly on my Sony Walkman, for which I'd saved the entire sixty-five dollars. Because I wasn't at the stage where I could discern what was cool or not, I tentatively asked my best friend James about Carey's album, and whether he loved it as much as I did.

'Mariah fucking Carey?' There was pity in his eyes. 'What are you, a homo?' I shuffled in my spot, unsure of the appropriate response. 'And what are those shorts you're wearing, by the way?' James said. 'Are they *Mango*?' I looked down at the imitation Mambo-brand shorts my mother had bought me from Best 'n' Less – the ones I reserved for special occasions, like the Fridays James and I went league tenpin bowling. What I had thought was cool – Mariah Carey, my imitation brand-label shorts – I now realised was a source of deep, deep shame. At least I was feeling it now.

'You can't go on listening to that shit,' James said, spraying Brut-33 deodorant into his eleven-year-old armpits. Driving to the bowling alley, James told his mother to put on several CDs for me: The Twelfth Man's *Wired World of Sports II* and Denis Leary's *I'm an Asshole*. Dennis Leary's song I could understand and enjoy, but as I'd been raised in a non-cricket household, The Twelfth Man went right over my head. He was boring. But because it was spoken word, all I needed to do was block it out, by privately looping Mariah Carey through my head.

*

Needless to say, there was an answer once I, as Mariah suggested, 'reached into my soul.' All of these things – the fashion parade; the gymnastics lessons; Mariah Carey; my lack of body hair; my almost religious commitment to the mid-'90s gameshow *Man O Man*, a male beauty pageant hosted by *Phantom of the Opera*'s Rob Guest – pointed towards a particularly aggressive form of homosexuality.

When puberty hit, boys prowled the schoolyard – reeking of armpits, penis and locker-room Lynx – on the hunt for anyone remotely queer to exercise their knuckles on. God knows how, but I passed the test. I learned which girls were supposedly attractive; I perfected my man-walk; and I had that rich baritone voice to hide behind. People chose to look beyond my involvement in the all-female clarinet ensemble and my art-class creations of semi-naked muscled Christ figures. Being Asian helped. People never suspected you could be a racial minority *and* gay. Of course you're not gay; you're *foreign*.

Still, the anxiety was constant. The whole time, I was busy convincing myself that I was infatuated with Helen, a girl from my extracurricular acting class. She was misanthropic, liked Radiohead, was obsessed with Jonny Greenwood and smelled nice. She had lovely feet. I had severe scoliosis and a Tori Amos rarities collection. In our locality, this was as close as the youth got to cutting-edge. A few months into our friendship, I sent Helen an anonymous Valentine's Day card with Elliott Smith lyrics scrawled all over it. She called my bluff and asked me out on a date during an online chat. I became flustered, confused, and – somehow knowing in my gut that this would be wrong – typed something like 'Uhmnothanksokaybye.' Then I made my online profile invisible. Knowing my teenage self, it's very likely I then spent the next few hours looking at homosexual pornography.

The next time I saw her, Helen had changed. She scowled at me a lot. I couldn't help but feel partially to blame. In fact, I felt lousy.

'What's the problem?' Mum asked one night, after she found me heaving and dripping snot all over the sofa. I was crying so hard I couldn't breathe. My mouth opened and closed, gasping and fish-like: all movement, no sound.

I couldn't even speak.

'*Yuk*?' Mum patted my shoulder comfortingly and smiled.

'I ha-ave sum-thi-ing,' I choked, 'to tell you.'

She looked concerned. 'Are you on drugs?'

I shook my head.

'You've gotten Rebecca pregnant.' Rebecca was my best high-school friend.

'Oh god, no!' I sobbed.

'Um …' Mum said, as though she was on a game show. 'I know, I know! You're *gay*.'

When I nodded, she put a hand to her chest, sighed and then laughed with relief.

'Well, what's wrong with that?' Mum asked. 'There's nothing wrong with being gay.'

I looked up at her, surprised. 'Really?'

'Gay people can't help it,' she said. 'It just means that something went wrong in the womb, that's all.'

*

After I came out, it was strange not having something to be constantly anxious about, so I chose to focus again on my body. I'd hovered around the 49-kilogram mark for most of my life, and I was sick of it. I hadn't grown taller or put on any weight since I'd left high school. My aim was to build some biceps, stack on some muscle and stop looking as though someone had draped skin over a skeleton. My metabolism was like a furnace. I would ingest veritable troughs of food, only to crap it all out minutes later. It made weight gain extremely difficult.

I sought advice from my friend Daniel – someone who was so aggressively heterosexual and manly that he once shat *on* a toilet seat by mistake – who had become noticeably beefier. When I went to hug him each time I saw him, it became increasingly difficult; he was becoming a truck. His advice was simple: go to the gym; invest in protein shakes. So I did exactly as he said: I joined the gym, worked out like a demon and swam laps every other day. If my life were a movie, this period would be a montage of protein shakes, scrambled eggs, bacon, bananas, bench presses, swimming laps and grunting. Sweat would trickle down my face.

About a month later, I'd put on five kilos. On a body size like mine, this was a conspicuous change. Exhilarated, I became adventurous with the protein shakes, blending stuff like milk, bananas, Milo, a tub of Milo dairy dessert, WeetBix and raw eggs into the protein mix. Five hours later, the resulting farts were indescribably rancid.

'Holy shit,' said my sister Tammy from the next room, choking. 'What is that *smell*?' The farts would not stop.

Later, when my boyfriend Scott had trudged back from work, sleep-deprived and tired, the farts had still not subsided. Tammy had opened all the windows and doors, gasping. By bedtime, my bowels were still putting on a musical, one with both an auditory and olfactory score. Sighing, Scott endeavoured to 'massage them out' of me by rubbing my stomach, rather than having me leak gas throughout the night. But a few hours later, it was still going.

'Benjamin,' Scott finally said. 'This is a new low. Even for you.' He said this firmly but gently, and in the dark I nodded, understanding. Then I farted. Groaning and waving his hands,

Scott got up and opened the windows and doors again. Tammy screamed – she could smell it from the next room. It was official: I was repulsive. But while my bowels continued to spasm, expand, then yawn out sulphurous gas into the night, I couldn't help but think, 'Being disgusting. That's manly, isn't it?'

You've Got a Friend

Whenever she gets lonely, my mother tells me that friends – real friends, genuine, bona-fide, authentic friends – are rare and hard to find. When you've spent the last thirty years working as a stay-at-home mother of five children, what time do you have to make friends? 'And what is a friend, anyway?' she asks. 'How does anyone find real friends?' She says this to draw attention to how fortunate I am – *You have many real friends, Benjamin, and you are lucky by comparison* – but it usually does nothing but depress the hell out of me. Most of the Christmas cards Mum receives nowadays aren't from friends, but businesses: dentists and chiropractors posting out inkjet print-outs en masse, with impersonal, fill-in-the-blank TOs and FROMs, followed by a reminder to make an appointment in the new year.

Still, every year without fail, Mum receives one Christmas card from an old friend in Ipoh, the regional Malaysian town where both women spent their childhoods. The two have corresponded for nearly fifty years, annual greetings sent across oceans, one for every year since they left primary school. The cards from Mum's Malaysian friend, Aunty Clara, have always been warm and affectionate, almost long-form letters in their loving attention to detail. A childless woman, Aunty Clara always asked how Mum's five children were and how she was coping with the divorce, insisting that Mum should visit

Malaysia soon, stressing that she always had spare beds. *Bring the kids*, she'd write. *I'd love to get to know them properly.*

Aunty Clara's Christmas cards always struck me as non-judgmental and snoop-free: just friendly hellos and gentle shout-outs to let Mum know she was thinking of her and – even if my mother didn't believe it – that God was watching over her. Aunty Clara finished each card with 'Yours in Christ.' Sometimes the cards would go a little further and slip in gentle proclamations about how blessed we all were, how Jesus sacrificed himself for our sins, and how we should never forget the blood he shed for us and the never-ending glory of it all.

The religious interjections were supposed to be subtle, but Aunty Clara's segues were a little too obvious. From details of her home life – to Jesus. From anecdotes about her dogs – to Jesus. From stories of her trip to Canada – to Jesus. As kids, Clara and my mother had both attended Ave Maria, a private Catholic convent school staffed by severe, straight-backed nuns. Clearly, the Christianity had stuck with Aunty Clara; Mum, not so much. 'I believe in a higher something,' Mum told me, 'but I'm not into, like, *God-God-God*. Sometimes I talk to God, but I don't need to go to church to do that.' Religion made some people go crazy, she said.

Despite the Christianity, Aunty Clara's Christmas cards never failed to make Mum smile and reminisce. She would read them out loud, before regaling us with stories of Ipoh and her childhood. Her family had been renowned, she told us – a clan of seven astonishingly beautiful children who turned heads on the street when they caught taxis to school. Photographs from that time show boys and girls – my aunties and uncles – with the kind of slick hairstyles and high cheekbones I imagined fuelled childhood crushes throughout the region. Modelling scouts would accost them on the street with their business cards.

As kids, the seven siblings would eat shaved-ice desserts from street stalls, and fruit so ripe and juicy that the flavour exploded in your mouth on impact. The best mangos in Australia, Mum told us, were as nothing compared to the most ordinary Malaysian ones. Over there, rambutans grew like apples and mangosteens sprouted like weeds. Hearing all this as a kid in the suburbs left me breathless. I imagined a tropical landscape where children spontaneously danced in the street, mothers burst into song, and families lived in tree-houses with pet orangutans who wore vests and served coconut juice in the shell. Malaysia: it was a place of unimaginable beauty and exoticism, where Mum was surrounded by friends, and nothing could go wrong.

*

We were adults when we visited Malaysia for the first time. Tammy, a photographer, had spent the past nine months trekking and working throughout South-East Asia, and was ready to come home. Mum, Michelle and I told her we'd rendezvous with her, and we planned to travel as a foursome, seeing for the first time where Mum had grown up. It had been a long time coming.

Mum picked up the phone and called Aunty Clara, who didn't even need to think about housing us: she immediately said yes, prompting an endless stream of *thank-you*s and *are-you-sure*s from my mother. '*Mm-sae gum haak-hae,*' Aunty Clara scolded my mother over the phone. There's no need to be so polite.

When we arrived, a fresh-faced and smiling Uncle Wayne and Aunty Clara received us at the arrivals lounge. 'Hello!' they said. 'Yes, yes: it's us!' Aunty Clara had a narrow, bespectacled face and wore her hair in a neat Cleopatra bob. Uncle Wayne never stopped grinning: with his white moustache, he resembled a happy cartoon field-mouse. They were one of those couples who seem immediately familiar, and they spoke fluent English interspersed with bursts of Cantonese, just like us. Mum ran into Aunty Clara's arms and began to cry.

'You're not going to cry!' Aunty Clara said, laughing and squeezing Mum. Turning to Michelle and me, she said, 'Your mother has always cried so easily! Even when we were children!'

It wasn't every day I encountered someone who even knew my mother, let alone someone who remembered details about her that I didn't. Surely that constituted a friend, I thought, and I felt happy for them.

We stayed in Kuala Lumpur for a couple of days, making sure we saw the capital before the half-day drive to Ipoh. Up on the observation deck of KL Towers, I realised I'd forgotten to wear my contact lenses or glasses, so the night-time skyline was an exquisite, shiny blur.

*

As the days went on, I began to feel as though Aunty Clara and Uncle Wayne were somehow in complete denial about Malaysia. We drove to the Batu Caves, a massive Hindu temple built into a limestone cliff-face. On the way, I asked Uncle Wayne what he thought about the Malaysian politician Anwar Ibrahim. He shook his head and whispered quietly: 'Sodomy. You know about him, huh?' I'd only read the basics of Malaysian politics, but I suggested that the charges against Ibrahim seemed to have been manufactured by a corrupt government. Uncle Wayne shrugged. 'Maybe the charges are made up,' he said. 'But every government is corrupt, right? What can you do?'

We drove past mosques, some plain, some exquisite. When Michelle asked what sort of buildings they were, both Aunty Clara and Uncle Wayne claimed not to know. 'Isn't it a mosque?' Tammy asked. This was met with uneasy silence, the kind children encounter when they blurt out truths they're not meant to know. Aunty Clara sat quietly, nervously stroking the crucifix that dangled from her neck. When we passed a billboard bearing the Malaysian flag, Michelle took the opportunity to change the subject.

'What about the crescent and the star?' she said. 'What's that?'

'You mean on the flag?' Uncle Wayne asked.

'The crescent is a symbol of Islam,' I ventured.

'And most Malaysians are Muslim,' Tammy said, 'so it makes sense that—'

'Oh, no-no, *no-no-no*,' Aunty Clara and Uncle Wayne interjected. 'That can't be what it means.' Between them, they started brainstorming alternative meanings. A crescent? On a flag? It must mean something else! Something about night-time or the sky, or space exploration of some kind. Definitely not anything Muslim; nothing to do with Islam.

When we got to the Batu Caves, Aunty Clara refused to come up. 'I'm okay,' she said, straining and smiling and shooing us with her hands. 'Go, go! Too slippery for me. And look at the grip on these shoes.' As we started climbing, Mum spoke in hushed, private tones while gripping the handrail. 'Just so you know, your aunty's not scared of the *steps*,' she said. 'It's because she's a devout Christian, and this place is …' She pointed to the giant sculpture of Murugan behind us, the Hindu war god. '*You know.*'

As we drove to Ipoh, Mum and Tammy asked how Aunty Clara and Uncle Wayne had first met. Immediately, the atmosphere became light and bashful. They were childhood sweethearts.

'Oh, you know what's really funny?' Aunty Clara asked, slapping her thighs and laughing. 'Did you know, that because Uncle Wayne was so dark as a teenager, many people thought he was a Muslim! Yes, it's true! I promise! Haha, look at him: this Chinese man, a Muslim! So funny, oh dear me, oh my.' She chuckled with deep, throaty laughter.

'And what about you, Aunty Clara?' Tammy said. 'When you first met him, did you mistake him for a Muslim guy too?'

'No!' Aunty Clara said. 'No, no, no. Not at *all*. If I even suspected that, I wouldn't have even said *hello*. I wouldn't be so *stupid*.' She was almost spat the word. 'Like my sister-in-law, Uncle Wayne's sister, going off and marrying a Muslim man. She even converted! Such a *stupid, stupid* woman. Stupid woman.' Aunty Clara said it again softly. 'So stupid.'

We shifted uncomfortably in the backseat.

*

When we reached Ipoh, we drove into a clippered, sectioned-off residential estate, where Aunty Clara and Uncle Wayne lived in a massive, peach-coloured house. Unlike other people who offered their homes as a mandatory kindness, Aunty Clara and her husband – Uncle Wayne – had the space. She had inherited money after her father, a politician, was spectacularly assassinated.

That inheritance, combined with Wayne's income and their lack of children, had secured them a mansion with an entire wing reserved for guests.

As soon as the Mercedes pulled into the driveway, dogs started barking. One was a small miniature something-or-other, a ferret–sausage hybrid with long toenails that appeared never to have been clipped. As a result, he was constantly tapping over his tiled enclosure like a gay showdog on Broadway. Mum and the girls would share one large room with trundle beds, while I slept in a single-sized room by myself. The first thing I noticed was a wooden crucifix blu-tacked to the wall next to a power-point. When I turned around, I saw the room's main decoration: a large poster that read, 'I AM THE BREAD, THE TRUTH AND THE LIFE.' It was a very literal poster. It featured a photograph of bread. All over the house was Jesus paraphernalia: magnets, framed paintings, pamphlets, wooden carvings that simply said 'GOD.'

That night, after everyone else had gone to bed, I overheard Aunty Clara and Mum gossiping outside on the sofa, talking about hard times, how women their age had become invisible, how each of them had coped over the years. 'You know how I remained strong?' Aunty Clara asked in Cantonese. 'I turned to God. When my father was assassinated by that crazy man, when my sister died of cancer, who was there for me? No one. No one but God.' She went in for the kill. 'You know what? You should come to church with me sometime.'

But it became clear that Mum had no intention of converting. When Aunty Clara spoke about church life at home, Mum's eyes glazed over. When Aunty Clara spoke about God in the car, Mum fell asleep. She couldn't help it. But it worked both ways.

When Mum spoke about her children's achievements, Aunty Clara trumped her with stories about her godchildren, who were lawyers, accountants and surgeons. A distance started to grow between them.

As we made our way through Ipoh, there were disappointments. Those renowned mangosteens were limp and slightly sour. We didn't see one rambutan, and the orangutans were on another Malaysian island completely. The legendary apartment where Mum grew up had been gutted and transformed into a Sony appliances store. 'She used to live here,' I explained to the annoyed staff, when Mum started taking photos of the shop's interior. At Ave Maria Convent School, Mum and Aunty Clara posed for photos until a stout, moustachioed female security guard came out and shooed us off.

Another day we went to a giant shopping mall, a multi-layered maze of glass, white concrete and chrome, the type of never-ending, sprawling complex that looks like an M.C. Escher and Joan Collins collaboration in hell. After a few minutes, we lost Mum.

'How could you have been so irresponsible?' Aunty Clara said when we returned without her. 'You always go shopping separately from your mother? Now she could be *anywhere*.'

'But she knows to meet us back here,' I said. 'We said if we lost each other, if there was an emergency—'

'It's an emergency now!' she said. 'Your mother! She's nowhere to be seen! How do you expect her to find her way around a place like this, huh?'

I was about to protest when Uncle Wayne interjected.

'*Ai-ya*, you don't know Malaysia,' he said, shaking his head. '*Anything* could happen. She could be *dead*.'

We searched the mall for ages. Eventually, Mum appeared with dozens of shopping bags, giggling and giddy, showing us photos she'd taken of all the store clerks who'd served her. When I told her it had been nearly an hour, she was dismissive.

'I lose track when I'm SKI-ing!' she said. 'Why keep track of the time when you can SKI?' SKI was her new favourite phrase. It stood for 'Spending the Kids' Inheritance.'

We walked to the carpark together, Mum leading the way with her shopping bags while we sulked and trailed behind her.

'Tell me,' Aunty Clara said, pulling me aside and whispering under her breath. 'Does your mother always spend money like this?' She tsked disapprovingly. 'She reminds me of my sister, always buying this and that. So many *things*, isn't it?'

Driving back to their house in Ipoh, I decided that I didn't much like Aunty Clara anymore. When Mum and I were left to ourselves, I started telling Mum about Aunty Clara's bitchiness, hoping she'd finally see her for what she was. To my surprise, Mum defended her. 'You don't know anything about this woman. She might not be perfect, but what friend is?' I blinked at her, not knowing what to say, then immediately felt like a brat. Who was I to criticise this couple who had invited us into their home and driven us halfway across the country? What was I doing, running down one of Mum's few good friends? What did I hope to achieve?

When they drove us to the airport, Aunty Clara and Uncle Wayne compounded my shame by forcing each of us to take a traditional red money-packet stuffed with cash. As we waited for the traffic to subside, Aunty Clara said out of nowhere, 'I have so many friends, you know. So, so many good friends. It doesn't matter who you are, if you're rich or poor, what race you are.

Anyone with a good personality, who has a nice heart, Aunty Clara will be your friend. So many friends.' She turned in her seat and smiled at Mum, showing all her teeth. 'As long as you are a Christian, I'll be your friend.'

Christmas was only a few weeks away, and I noticed that none of the shopping centres or restaurants we'd visited had decorated their interiors for the season. I had almost forgotten we were in a Muslim country. Maybe we'd been living with Aunty Clara and Uncle Wayne for too long. As we drove towards the airport, I wondered how many Christmas cards each of us would receive that year, and from whom.

God Camp

At seven years old, I already knew I was headed straight for hell. None of my primary-school teachers ever said so directly – never pointed an accusatory finger at me and said, 'You're going to hell, Benjamin' – but all our Bible lessons pointed to the same conclusion. If you hadn't been baptised, if you didn't take Holy Communion, if you didn't go to church on Sunday, it was simple: you'd end up burning in Satan's furnaces for the rest of eternity. Eternity. It seemed like a pretty long time.

At school, we had celebrated Baptism Certificate Day, when all the Year 3 students were asked to bring copies of their christening documents; our teacher hung them around the room, like tinsel. I was the only student who didn't have one. The other kids looked at me, concerned.

'Mum,' I said after school. 'I need to get baptised or I'm going to hell. We all are.'

'You don't need to be baptised,' she said.

'You're not listening to me. We *all* need to be baptised. We *all* need to go to church. Because it won't be nice when I'm the only one in heaven and I have to think about the rest of you burning in hell's fiery lakes forever.'

She told me to wait until I was twelve years old; then I would be in a better position to make up my own mind about religion.

'But what if I *die* before then? Have you thought of that?

What if I'm eleven years old and get run over by a car and end up rotting in hell because you didn't baptise me?'

'Well, you wouldn't go to hell. You're only a kid,' she said. Then, sensing my worry, she added, 'And even if you did, I'm sure they would treat you better down there. Because you're so *cute*!'

Every morning before class, we filed into our daily worship session. Devotions covered a broad range of topics: forgiveness; receiving compliments gracefully; documented Satanic possessions. Music came courtesy of the school band, a misfit hodge-podge of whichever musically inclined students were available that week: recorder, baritone clarinet, piccolo, French horn, bongos. One of my favourite songs was 'The Blind Man,' a participation-based hymn made up of verses featuring men suffering various afflictions – blindness, deafness, paralysis – searching for Christ to show them the way.

'The blind man sat by the road and he cried!' we sang. 'The blind man sat by the road and he cried!' The final verse simply involved shouting 'The Blind Man!' followed by frenzied, rhythmic clapping to fill in the gaps. Years later, singing the same song in high school, it struck me as undignified and mean, implying the blind man was not only vision-impaired, but also had some form of palsy that made him clap in a wild, uncontrollable fashion. But as a Christian-hearted seven-year-old, I dug the clapping as much as I dug Jesus.

*

Our school prided itself on its discipline and tradition, and like all Christian schools, it was built on the fundamental tenet of original sin. Young people could not be trusted, and had to be reformed. The centrepiece of this was the Year 10 camping program, in which students were shipped out into the bush for a month. They called it 'survival camp'; returning to your parents alive was the goal. It was located in a cluster of cabins owned by the school and christened Mount Kilmore, set in the ominously named region of Blackbutt, a winding two-hour bus ride away from the school. People vomited going up that mountain. Parts of the incline were so steep that buses and cars snaked around the roads in sickening U-turns, dangerously close to the lip of the cliffs.

I was still a devout ten-year-old when my eldest sister, Candy, went to Mount Kilmore. We visited her on Parents' Day, the halfway point of the camp, when family members were invited to check up on their children. It was the only time campers were allowed junk food, brought in by family members. When our red Ford Cortina finally found the campground gate, we searched the horizon for Candy. Fourteen-year-olds in flannelette and denim cut-offs slouched towards the car in slow motion, arms stretched out in front of them, gaunt. 'Do you have anything to eat?' they droned. 'Did you bring snacks?' We wound up our windows, slowly and carefully, until they walked away weakly, their arms still outstretched and their eyes vacant.

When we finally found Candy, she was two shades darker, suntanned and dirt-stained. Although she seemed happy enough, some things about the camp horrified us.

'So,' she said. 'Do you want to see the furnace where we incinerate our used pads?'

My faith was shaken when she showed us the thing. Between the starving youth and half-charred tampons – all black and red like badly burnt steak chunks – there clearly wasn't any god.

*

By the time I was in Year 10, there were roughly 150 of us, and we went to camp in four groups. As I was in the last group to leave, I'd accumulated a lot of correspondence from friends who'd gone first. 'There is nothing out here,' they wrote. 'Nothing.' They'd plead for us to send lollies or chips, warning us to conceal the contraband in boxes of tissues or tampons. All parcels had to be opened in front of the camp staff, they told us, and if banned items were discovered, the student would be 'punished.' They wrote the word with quotation marks – 'punished' – as if it meant something different out there.

Some letters contained horror stories: how Betty rolled off a cliff and was air-lifted to hospital; how Selena reportedly had sex with a camp counsellor who looked like Chopper Read; how Callum almost died from an asthma attack; how three girls had swum in a seemingly pristine creek, only to find a dead cow in the water; how Darren had chased Taylor around with an axe, prompting the staff to lock all cabin doors while Darren prowled outside, brooding.

While my friends were going insane out in the woods, back at home I was going insane in my own modest way. I had begun to have acute anxiety attacks. These were like nothing I'd ever experienced before: paralysing sessions of irrational panic that left me unable to breathe or think. My siblings and I share a history of bizarre and transformative puberties, and between us we had an impressive repertoire of adolescent illnesses: deep depression, spontaneous hairloss, stomach ulcers. Some nights I'd find myself pinned to the mattress, sweating and dizzy with fear that I'd be possessed by the Devil and hurt myself or a family member. I kept away from all sharp objects. When my mother served me steak, I ate it with a blunt butter knife. When she used a cleaver in the kitchen to hack up pork bones, I'd lock myself in my room and put on my headphones, blocking out the thunks of metal slamming against bone. For me, survival camp was a horrifying prospect: one of the mandatory items we had to take was a freshly sharpened Swiss Army knife. My friends had also told me that one of the first things they gave you upon arrival was a machete.

*

We headed out in the dead of winter. Once there, we filed off the bus, shivering, and unloaded our bags. The camp staff stood in an unmoving line, watching us silently, the way sergeants inspect new military grunts. We'd heard so much about these people over the last few months that they'd assumed a mythic quality. Each was instantly recognisable from our friends' descriptions. Moustachioed Pastor Foster carried a rifle over his shoulder and was constantly followed by a pair of huskies, who would growl at newcomers. He spoke with his hands on his hips, and was known for enforcing a Reich-like discipline. 'Welcome to survival camp, folks,' he said. 'Leave your bags here. First things first. Everyone into the Devotion Room.'

The Devotion Room was an old stable, and it smelled like leather, straw and pony shit. 'If God is on our side,' we sang, examining the gigantic old knives pinned to the wall, 'if God is on our side, who can be against us?' As we sang tunelessly, we checked out the remaining staff members.

True to our friends' accounts, twenty-something Mr Dane had the biggest nose we'd ever seen; it looked prosthetic: rubbery and removable. Although it was the middle of an unforgiving winter, Mr Dane would wear skin-tight stubbies every day without fail; whenever he lifted his legs, we flinched. Miss

Phillips was clearly in love with Mr Dane, and wore her hair in a daring, come-hither bowl-cut. With her meaty, androgynous face and farm-hardened, utilitarian breasts, she was probably considered a catch in Blackbutt. She smiled *constantly*, a tic that was meant to be welcoming, but took on a sinister quality as the camp progressed.

Mr and Mrs Barry were the elders of Mount Kilmore. They owned a property nearby, and were the most devout Christians of them all. My sister Candy had told me that Mrs Barry had declared the Joan Osborne song 'One of Us' blasphemous. Later, I would find myself discussing horoscopes, fortune telling and Nostradamus with some girls at camp. Overhearing us, Mrs Barry screamed and decried Nostradamus as a Satan worshipper. She had a lazy eye that became irritable when the weather turned cold: you could never tell whether she was giving you a conspiratorial wink or just needed some eyedrops. These people would be our guardians for the next month.

'Let us pray to God,' Pastor Foster said. And for the first time in Devotion, every single one of us did.

*

Most of the camp was pleasant enough. We got up at six o'clock every morning, woken by a clanging bell, and raised the Australian flag in the middle of a dark paddock. We were like the Amish: baking bread, feeding chickens, showering naked with corrugated iron sheets between us for privacy. We hand-washed our laundry in metal drums with giant levers, then squeezed it through two giant rolling pins stuck together. Out in the stables, we'd throw fresh, steamy horse-turds at one another, giggling. It was very wholesome.

But as the weeks went on, the mood became glum. For 'fun,' we would be separated into groups for lantana-culling competitions, given blunt machetes and told to hack into a massive cluster of weeds and branches. The winning team's reward was a single Mars Bar, to be shared among us. The girls were becoming lazy. Exhausted by the long walk to burn their tampons and pads in the furnaces, they started using their kitchen stoves instead.

Something also seemed to be wrong with my lungs: I couldn't breathe without hearing a jagged rumbling. On every hike, my friend Chantelle and I would be last in line. Together, we struggled up hills and lost sight of the others.

'Hurry up, slow-pokes!' Miss Phillips said. 'What's taking you so long?'

Chantelle gasped for air, her mouth opening and closing desperately.

'Ben?' she said. 'I can't breathe.'

I laughed. 'That's funny, Chantelle,' I said. 'I can't breathe either.'

'No, I mean it: I really can't breathe.'

Less than a minute later, Chantelle was on the ground, unconscious, her limbs seizing up and spasming. Her feet were rigid and pigeon-toed. Her hands were contorted, like she was possessed.

'What do we do, *what-do-we-do?*' someone asked. 'Is she going to die?'

'Chantelle, has this happened before?' Miss Phillips said, panicked but still stiffly smiling, slapping Chantelle's face repeatedly. 'Stay awake, talk to us.'

Chantelle's eyes were open, but we couldn't see her pupils – just the whites. It gave me the creeps.

'Here,' someone said, passing over a Ventolin inhaler. 'Give her this.'

'Was anyone around her when she fell over?' Miss Phillips said. 'Ben, you were with her. Did she say anything?'

Guiltily, I drew a circle in the dirt with my shoe. 'I don't know.'

Chantelle eventually recovered, but the rattle in my own chest turned out to be a lung infection. One of the staff members drove me into 'town,' where a doctor prescribed me penicillin. Drugged up and half-asleep on the drive back to camp, my anxiety attacks came back. I had the sinking feeling something terrible was going to happen.

*

When I got back to camp, girls were screaming. Boys sat on their porches, captivated by the show that had just begun. In the middle of the quadrangle, Pastor Foster was having a showdown with one of my classmates, Rosie. Of all of us, Rosie had been having the most trouble adjusting to camp life, and had become moody and difficult with the staff.

I sat down with a group of boys, who explained that Rosie had been out on a hike that morning when a stray dog started following her, sniffing around in a friendly manner. Rosie was charmed, and christened him Digger. It was the first time anyone had seen her smile at camp. She had brought him back to the cabins with her, and now Digger stood behind her on a makeshift leash. He looked lean and ratty: part dog, part dingo. Behind Pastor Foster, his puff-ball huskies growled at the newcomer menacingly. Both parties had to struggle to hold the dogs back.

'*I hate you!*' Rosie screamed at Pastor Foster. 'Just fucking *die!*'

'You get that mongrel away from my dogs,' Pastor Foster said, 'or I'll shoot it. My rifle is close by, and I'd have no hesitation killing the mongrel.'

'He's not a mongrel!' Rosie said. 'Look at your stupid gay dogs!'

Everyone nodded silently to one another. They were pretty gay.

'Rosie, we won't tolerate that sort of language here.'

'Go ahead and shoot him then! Let everyone see you for the monster you are!'

Pastor Foster glared at her, and gave a single nod: he was getting his rifle. Everyone tensed up. Mrs Barry started blinking more rapidly. Miss Phillips's eyes darted, and she smiled wider and wider in panic. Crying, Rosie took Digger by the lead and tied him to a nearby post. Purple in the face, tears streaming down her cheeks, she stormed around the camp's tool sheds, until she finally emerged with what she wanted: a massive metal lance, at least six feet long, with a hook on the end.

'I'll kill Pastor Foster,' she said. 'I'll ram this through his ugly head.'

After we had calmed Rosie down, Digger the dog finally wandered off, confused and rejected. Rosie sat, slumped and defeated, by the camp gate. Like the blind man in our morning hymns, she sat by the road and she cried.

*

As time went on, my lung infection got worse, and people started to question whether I'd make it to Solo. Designed to be the culmination of all our previous hikes, Solo involved trekking in an all-male or all-female group. At designated spots, within 'screaming distance' of one another in case of emergencies, each camper was left to spend the night alone. When the penicillin finally kicked in and my phlegm cleared up, I was deemed fit enough to join the others.

On the big day, as we marched through the sloping mountains, Mr Dane talked us through everything we'd learned on previous hikes: how to make a fire; how to find and chop kindling; how to make a tent with our water-proof mats and string. We nodded uncertainly.

As we hiked on, someone noticed we were missing something. 'Mr Dane?' he asked, 'Where are the shovels?' We carried shovels so that we could dig makeshift toilets. Defecating on the side of the road, or next to a tree, where locals might step in it, was considered poor form. 'Oh, sugar!' Mr Dane said. 'I knew I forgot something. You men will just have to be careful where you do your business. Cover it with dirt or something.'

When it came my turn to be left alone, I was dropped off near a creek. It had recently rained, which made it close to impossible to start a fire. For dinner, I ate powdered milk straight out of the packet; the dryness caked my mouth like powdered chalk. I ate baked beans and soup unheated, and put the empty cans back in my hiking pack. Because I didn't have a shovel, I took a crap next to a tree. I didn't bother covering it with dirt. Still weak from my lung infection, I was too lazy to construct a shelter, so I crawled into my sleeping bag, pulled my waterproof mat around me and whimpered for the next few hours.

In the middle of the night, I woke up with a start, seized by the idea that the Devil was here, had found my machete and was lurking in the scrub. There was an awful rustling in the trees. *This is real, this is happening,* I thought – no amount of screaming would save me now. Suddenly, there was a rush of violent, noisy flapping above my head, and I could hear myself shrieking. Frightened half to death, it took me ages to realise that a flock of wild geese had flown over and landed in the creek next to me. Anyone within screaming distance would have heard me.

The next morning, while taking a long, draining piss against a tree, I thought vaguely, 'This ground is so *squishy*.' I had stepped in my own shit. It was time to go home.

*

On our last night at Mount Kilmore, we celebrated our survival by killing an animal. The mood was jubilant, and everyone went feral. A whole hog had been brought in to roast, and we'd wrapped it in banana leaves, buried it under hot coals and waited like savages for it to cook. Callie, the only vegetarian, staged an animal rights protest with a sign that proclaimed 'JESUS DIED: BUT WE DIDN'T EAT HIM.' But we were hungry, and they'd promised us gravy.

The next day, there was a thorough audit and clean-up of the campgrounds. Floorboards were swept, kitchens sterilised. In the girls' cabin, a fire was lit in the kitchen to burn the rest of their garbage. By the time I visited, the girls' enthusiasm for the fire had grown, and they were fuelling it with whatever they could find: plastic bottles, Bibles, sugar. Each substance made the fire react in a new and fascinating way. Finally, they threw in a chair. Not a wooden one, but a chair you might find in a café, with metal legs, foam stuffing and a vinyl seat. The flames crept up, engulfing the legs and finally the seat itself, creating a tower of flame as tall as us. We stared at it in reverent silence.

*

The purpose of the camp had been to reconnect with God. But after thirty days in the wilderness, none of us needed a pastor to tell us about God and the Devil, or to describe the kingdom of heaven, or tell us what hell was like. Getting off the bus and seeing our parents again, it felt like we'd been to hell and back already. It was a place we knew well. We could have drawn you a map.

The Pretenders

In my first year of primary school, our class stripped down to our underwear, covered ourselves in black body paint and pretended to be Aborigines. We were all scheduled to appear in the annual talent showcase, and because there weren't any actual Aboriginal kids in the class, we opted for blackface instead. Students were split into two groups: the tallest half would play Aboriginal parents; the short kids would be their children. As the tiniest boy in the group, I was given the role of a native infant. It was easy work, and involved pretending I was asleep by laying my head in the lap of my tall friend John, who would play my father. We'd then all sing the lullaby 'Carra Barra Wirra Canna' – a song we assumed was traditional – written by a man named Rolf Harris – a man we assumed was Aboriginal. On the evening of the showcase, our parents filed into the assembly hall, and students and teachers huddled backstage, running through the choreography one last time.

'Sing it soothingly,' one of teachers reminded us. 'Remember, Aborigines sing lullabies to their children too, just like your parents at home.'

Behind the curtains, John and I took our position at the front of the stage, in amongst the cardboard shrubs and fauna. It happened all at once: the curtains opened, Mrs Semmler started playing the piano, and the stage lights shone with an unexpectedly intense heat, which immediately made our body paint sticky and toxic-smelling. 'There's a lake in South Australia,' the Aboriginal parents sang, 'little lake with lovely name.' Then the rest of us – the Aboriginal kids – rubbed our eyes, as though we were waking from a long Dreamtime sleep. 'And the story woven round it,' we sang sleepily, 'from the piccaninnies came.' Parents cooed.

When we finished, the applause seemed to go on forever. From my prime position at the front of the stage, I lapped it all up. For days afterwards, I was on a high, convinced that show business was my destiny.

Things soured a year later, when my friend Shelley and I were cast as wolves in the school production of *Noah's Ark*. Mum and I made snouts and ears out of cardboard, sewed pantyhose stuffed with cotton onto grey leggings, and added dental floss for a tail. Unlike the other animals, the wolves were fortunate enough to have speaking parts.

'We're so hungry!' Shelley announced to the crowd.

'We just want to howl!' I said.

'Wahhh-ooooh!' we cried out in unison.

Everyone applauded and laughed. That was enough for me to immediately want to do it again, and it was difficult to accept my moment had passed. Because it was a combined year-level performance, all the animals were portrayed by a new set of students after intermission. As I watched them from backstage, reciting their lines, I could barely conceal my contempt for the new wolf in his cheap grey tracksuit get-up, which was clearly a Salvation Army purchase. He didn't care about his speaking role; that much was obvious. He had no respect for his craft, and this just made me sick. *Who did he think he was?* I thought. *And since when did wolves have cotton-wool stumps for tails?*

When we got home, I scanned the program frantically, only to find my name had been mistakenly omitted and replaced by the other male wolf. His name appeared twice; mine was nowhere to be seen. The worst thing was, he wouldn't even have cared.

'What's wrong?' Mum asked me, when she saw my bottom lip trembling.

'Nothing's wrong,' I said. 'I said nothing's wrong! Everything's okay! Nothing's wrong! Just shut up! *SHUT UP.*'

Then I threw the program into the corner of the room, started punching the sofa and broke into open and shameless weeping and howling – a reaction that surprised even me. Clearly, they'd cast me as the right animal.

*

After a few years, I was set: if I hadn't scored a speaking role on *Home and Away* by the age of fifteen, I would consider myself a failure. Macaulay Culkin had been ten when *Home Alone* was released, so I figured fifteen was a reasonable, realistic sort of goal. Success by the age of twelve would have been ideal, but I lived in a regional area away from television studios and thought it would be wise to allow myself some breathing room, mainly to avoid setting myself up for disappointment. For the next few years, I followed *Home and Away* closely. What was striking was how young the actors were. In fact, they were nearly my age: pregnant Sophie, crying Sally, brooding Jack, doe-eyed Chloe. The fact that none of these actors was Asian didn't seem to register at the time.

At school, I threw myself into drama. We learned everything, from the history of the Greek tragedies, to the parallels between

Commedia dell'arte and *Are You Being Served?* Our bearded drama teacher, Mr Mallory Mallory – who had changed his name by deed poll – was a gloriously fat man who always dressed in black. In any other context, he would have resembled a homosexual bondage master, but at school, he was a man of the theatre. When mad at us, he would take off one of his canvas shoes and throw it in our direction, bellowing. 'You stupid child!' he'd scream. We'd all laugh. Once, a student joked to another about how fat Mr Mallory was, before realising the shadow behind him was not created by a passing cloud, but by Mr Mallory himself. After a moment of silence passed between them, Mr Mallory spoke in a low and dangerous tone.

'Do you know,' he asked, almost whispering, 'what would happen if I *sat* on you?'

Trembling, the student said he did not.

'YOU WOULD DIE!'

The students ran away, terrified. Moments like these made us adore and fear him in equal measure.

For one of our first drama lessons, we wore neutral masks and black robes, before being herded out into the green area near the sound shell, the school's disused outdoor amphitheatre. We started by lying on the ground, before Mr Mallory told us to rise, slowly, as though emerging from a deep hibernation. Soon, we were told to explore one another's spaces, touching one another's bodies, as though it was the first time we'd encountered another human being. We were like black slugs slithering and squirming slowly towards and onto one another.

By the time we were pretending to fly make-believe kites, I could see through my mask's eye-slits that the woodwork jocks were staring at us from their studio, laughing and making masturbating gestures. *Wankers*, they were saying to each other. *What a bunch of wankers.*

'Now you are in the wind!' Mr Mallory told us. 'You *are* the kite! Become one with the kite!'

The jocks laughed even harder.

'Fly!' Mr Mallory told us. 'Fly in the breeze! Stretch out those kite-arms and give yourself to the *wind*.'

Through my neutral mask, I could see that the woodwork guys were almost helpless now, slapping each other on the back and impersonating our exercises. *You'll see*, I thought to myself, my black robe flapping and dancing in the wind. *When I'm famous, you'll all be sorry.*

*

Shortly after my fourteenth birthday, I came across an advertisement for a local modelling and acting agency. 'INTERESTED IN AN ACTING CAREER? SERIOUS ABOUT MODELLING? Our talent agency was established in 1980! We represent talent of all ages! If you're serious about your career, see us today!' When I rang their offices, they told me a fee was involved if I wanted to be represented by them – or to 'be on their books,' as they called it. I gathered up my pocket money, then lobbied my dad for the rest.

'I don't really understand what this money's for,' he said, counting out the fifty-dollar notes carefully in his study.

'You have to hand over money to *make* money,' I explained. 'Aren't you a businessman? Remember when you paid for my gymnastics lessons? Or my clarinet classes? This is the same thing, except this will be my *job*. There will be *returns*.'

He looked at me sceptically. Perhaps it was that my orthodontic plate made me look like a duck, or the blossoming acne
that was spreading over my cheeks like a rash. But something
probably told him his child wasn't going to be an actor. Or at
least, not a successful one.

Still, Dad drove me to the talent agency a few days later,
where we were greeted by the agency's founder, a pert, powder-
puff of a woman called Faye. In her office, black and white
photos of young, handsome Caucasian teenagers smiled at us.

'Well!' Faye said, smiling broadly. 'I'm just so glad you con-
tacted us! It's so rare to have *Orientals* in our catalogue. You're
all just so hard to find!'

The way she spoke about it, Faye made me feel that she'd
been waiting to find me her entire career – some rare, ethnic
treasure. And here I was! Right inside her office! How about
that!

'You know, it'd be such a thrill to have you on our books,
Benjamin. A real *thrill*. Having diversity on the screen is so
important, don't you think?' And while I hadn't given it a thought
before, I realised that I absolutely agreed. Suddenly, this wasn't
just about me; this was about the future of diversity in television.
What we were doing in this room was important.

At the end of our meeting, she gave us directions to a photo
studio, where they'd take my photos for a few hundred dollars.
In the studio, posing in front of the lights, my orthodontic
plate made it difficult for me to smile properly. When I collected
the photos a few days later, I winced slightly at the results:
blotchy skin, weird mouth, hair like a toilet brush, only one
eye with an actual eyelid. Even the receptionist seemed to
notice. 'Don't worry,' she said consolingly. 'People in casting

don't look at the photos *that* closely. They only want a *rough* idea of what you look like.'

*

I'd collected several brochures from Faye's office, one of which was for private acting classes. The academy was based in Brisbane, but they also ran satellite classes on the Sunshine Coast, where I lived. At my first, free introductory lesson, all the other students sat on the stairwell's railings, gossiping and waiting for the doors to open. Everyone wore the same thing: a dark blue polo top, onto which the academy's logo was embossed: the letter 'A,' bordered by twisting film reels to form a classy and timeless emblem. I kept my distance from everyone else until an over-whelmingly friendly girl approached me, eating biscuits from the box.

'Hi!' she said. 'You go to my school. I'm Julie!'

'Oh, hey. I'm Ben.'

Julie and I shook hands. A car pulled up and two adults – a man and a young woman – got out, carrying props and folders.

'That's Anthony, and that's Natalya,' Julie said, pointing. 'They're so awesome. You'll love them.'

Anthony, the academy's founder, was a sturdily handsome man with rugged features. With his square chin and wavy brown hair, he was like the missing Baldwin brother. As well as teach-ing, he'd already featured in several television commercials, and in a community theatre productions of *The Boys*, in which he'd played a rapist. Teaching alongside him was Natalya, a much younger woman whose black hair, large head, bug eyes and striped stockings made her look like she'd wandered off a Tim Burton set.

At the start of the class, we formed a circle. 'Everyone, I'd like you all to welcome our newest student over here,' Anthony said, smiling with fantastically straight teeth that made me want to keep my mouth shut. 'Do you prefer Benjamin or Ben?'

I mumbled my standard response: whatever was easier.

'Now, before we start, we should introduce Ben to the academy's ground rules. Would someone like to explain to Ben what the Safety Net is?'

Everyone put up their hands, but Anthony chose Stefan, a skinny blond boy with hair so conditioned it formed a permanent halo over his head. Before the class began, he had performed solos from *Les Misérables*, shoulders raised, hands by his side, moist eyes looking to the horizon, just to warm up.

'The Safety Net,' Stefan said theatrically, 'means that in the academy, there's never any paying out or putting down, no matter what you think.'

Homo, I thought to myself.

'There's only just total support!' he said.

Sounds gay.

'So no one says anything unless it's *encouraging*,' Natalya added, as though she could read my mind. She looked directly at me, stern but smiling. I looked at my feet.

'Whatever exercises we do, don't be afraid to take a risk and really go for it,' Anthony added. 'Everything that works in drama is about taking a risk, you know.'

Every week from then on, our starry-eyed group of twenty would file into the old church hall and start breathing exercises and trust games. As I became more involved in the classes, the group became bigger and bigger. Remembering what it was like to be the new guy in the room, I'd greet the new members warmly. Like Clyde, a boy with home-cut hair and the hurt brown eyes of an abused dog.

'I've come here because my mother says I have low self-esteem,' Clyde told us at his first lesson. 'She thought this could be good for me … but whatever.'

In class, Clyde was riveting to watch. 'Well, why don't you go fuck yourself,' he'd say in improvisation exercises. Other times, he'd launch into even darker characters. 'I could fucking *kill you* if I wanted to,' he'd say, grabbing Stefan's collar during a theatre-sports exercise. Sometimes, in the middle of an improvisational skit, he'd violently lash out at the props, destroying them, screaming, 'This is all fucking shit, this is fucked and I hate it!'

'Whoa,' we'd say. 'Time out, time out!'

Clyde would look around, bewildered. 'That was okay, wasn't it?' he'd ask. 'It was my character. You understand, right?'

*

Academy showcases were held in Brisbane, and industry professionals – producers, directors, casting agents – were invited along every year as VIPs. After performing in a subversive rewrite of *Snow White*, I was signed up by a Brisbane agent, absolutely hand-picked. I'd come home from acting classes elated, another new skill-set under my belt, pick up my pet mouse, Humphrey, from his outdoor cage and tour the garden, pretending we were explorers in a television show: me and my anthropomorphic rodent. Together, we'd venture into dangerous and dramatic situations, for which I'd win both Emmys and Golden Globes.

'Things are looking up,' I told Humphrey. 'Things are looking *okay*.'

Through my Brisbane agent, I was called to an audition – three hours away – at Warner Brothers Movie World, a theme park on the Gold Coast that also functioned as a Hollywood movie studio. *A real audition.* All I knew was that it was a kung-fu film set in Singapore, and that although it was a small role, it was a speaking part – the big time. My brother agreed to drive me there, three hours out of his way, and I was jittery the whole trip.

As I stood in line for the auditions, theme-park rides thundered above my head. Standing in the beating sun and fanning myself with a photocopied script, I watched the rollercoasters, partly wishing I was spending the day on them, before reminding myself that all actors made sacrifices for their art. Reading over the script again, I knew the lines off by heart, but they still made no sense to me whatsoever.

When I finally got to the front of the audition line, I was directed into a dark, air-conditioned room, where a producer and director had positioned a video camera to record our screen tests.

'Hey, yo trip,' I recited, in front of the casting crew. 'Checkin' dis out and lookin' at da skematic, I can't tell you fo' sure!' I fumbled, forgetting my lines. 'Uhm …'

'Why don't you start again?' the director said.

I tried again, only to forget my lines in the same place. Partly, I was distracted by my own face, blown up in the monitor. At that moment, I had the strangest feeling that the person up there didn't have the same star-quality I saw in my mind, or when I posed in front of my darkened bathroom mirror.

'I'm really sorry,' I mumbled.

'That's okay. Perhaps try it again,' the producer said. 'But this time, do it with a stronger Asian accent.'

'Asian accent?'

'Well, the character's Asian, right? And you sound ... well, normal.'

I never heard back from them after that.

*

Storms arrived in the week that followed and the rain never let up. Outside, wind howled like a constant scream. Because Humphrey wasn't allowed indoors, I set his cage on a moat-ringed island of bricks so he wouldn't drown. As the rain pelted down, I became lazy and tried to avoid going out in the wet to feed him every day. Eventually, I just left some pieces of bread in his cage, which I figured would sustain him for at least a week.

At the acting academy, all the students were tense and anxious, and we'd arrive to class soaking wet. Showcase auditions were taking place again, and there were far fewer monologue spaces up for grabs. Scoring a monologue slot was one of the most important things you could do in the academy. It meant you'd get more face-time with the VIPs and a greater chance of being cast in a TV show or commercial. Competition was going to be fierce, since enrolments all over the state were at record highs. We sat in rows, watching one another's performances, audition-ing for academy staff we'd never encountered to ensure there wasn't any bias. I'd prepared a monologue from the movie *Twelve Monkeys*, a role for which Brad Pitt had been recently nominated for an Oscar. It was about germs.

'Eighteenth century, no such thing,' I announced, my eye twitching. 'Nada. Nothing. No one ever imagined such a thing. No sane person. Ah-uh-huh.' I leapt off the stage and leered at the audition panel. One of them arched an eyebrow at me before scrawling notes. 'Along comes this doctor – ah-ah-ah

– Semmelweiss, Semmelweiss. He's trying to convince people, well doctors mainly, that there's teeny, tiny invisible bad things called *germs* that get into your body – and, uh-huh-uh – make you sick.'

Anthony came to class the following week and announced the names of the two students who had scored monologue performances at the showcase. I wasn't one of them. As everyone else started celebrating and commiserating, Anthony gave me a look. During the break, he asked me to join him outside, away from the other students.

'What's going on?' he asked. 'Out of everyone who auditioned, I thought you would have been a shoo-in. The auditioner said you'd botched your lines.'

I suddenly felt very small.

'I didn't botch my lines,' I said. 'The character's a paranoid schizophrenic.'

'Well, maybe that didn't come across,' Anthony said. 'Whatever happened, I'm disappointed. Not disappointed in you; just disappointed in what's happened.'

When I got home that night, I felt like I was going to spew. Mum greeted me at the door, biting her lip.

'Mum?'

'I've got some bad news,' she said.

Somehow, I thought to myself, she knew about what had happened. Perhaps Anthony had telephoned her and discussed it, and called for an emergency intervention to resuscitate my dying acting career. Maybe he had told her that I was too important to give up on, that my family members should pool their funds and send me to the intensive training camps for actors they held every summer.

'Humphrey's dead,' she said. 'I found him this afternoon.'

I stood there unblinking.

'He drowned. I found him when I was taking out the bins. There was a mouldy piece of bread next to him. I think he starved to death.'

The storm had been raging for the past fortnight now, and I'd only fed him once. She didn't say it accusingly, but I knew what she was getting at. Our bargain had been that while I wasn't allowed a dog, I was able to have a small mouse, so long as Mum had nothing whatsoever to do with it. It was wholly my responsibility. I thought of Humphrey out there in the storm, his cage slowly filling up with water, utterly forgotten, the bread rotting next to him, dying alone, no one to remember him.

'*Humphrey*,' I whispered, under my breath. I paused for dramatic effect. 'Should we bury him?'

'I'm not sure,' Mum said. 'He really stinks, and it's still raining.'

We decided to bury him the next day.

That night, in the shower, I pulled out my orthodontic plate and tried to cry – '*Humphrey!*' – but even after summoning all the techniques I'd learned so far, it just wasn't going to happen. That was the sign of a bad actor: not being able to cry.

Months after the showcase, Anthony and Natalya told us that because the academy's enrolments were swelling so quickly, they wouldn't be able to personally teach regional classes like ours anymore. New local recruits would take care of us instead, all of whom were highly trained professionals. We felt abandoned.

The new teachers weren't much older than we were. 'Today, we are going to learn about American accents,' the new female teacher said, all firm breasts and white teeth. She was the complete opposite of black-haired Natalya, and we decided that we hated her. 'Accents are important for you guys to master, because a lot of the movies and television series being made locally are actually American. Look at *Flipper*!' For the rest of that evening, we recited monologues from *Party of Five* – the episode where Bailey is an alcoholic.

*

Years later, after I'd abandoned every single acting ambition I'd ever had, I accompanied my sister Michelle to an audition for a television commercial promoting the sandwich chain Subway. Whoever was cast in the various roles on offer – young chick, feckless boyfriend, corporate businesswoman – would earn an easy $2000 for dancing to a James Brown soundtrack. Byron, a friend of mine, was filming the casting reels. My sister was poor and enthusiastic, so I gave her a lift and helped her fill in forms about her dress measurements in the queue. Around us, women dressed for the corporate businesswoman role eyed each other's clipboards discreetly, or nervously asked one another questions. 'So, what sort of dancing do they want us to do? Do they just want us to go crazy, you think? Gyrate, maybe? Or something more subtle?'

Suddenly, the sliding doors of the audition room opened.

'Sorry,' Byron said to a woman around the corner. 'Excuse me?'

Sheepishly, she walked back towards us, her high-heels in her hands.

'Would you be able to practise your dancing somewhere else? We can see you through the window, and we don't want that in the footage.'

'Oh, sorry!' the woman said, creeping around the building. 'Sorry, sorry, sorry!' She laughed.

'That's okay. Keep practising. Practising is good,' Byron said. 'Just ... not there.'

When the doors closed again, the woman turned to us.

'I just think it's always good to have a bit of a run-through before these things,' she said, 'don't you?'

There was a faint odour of desperation about her. It was both familiar and repellent, and reminded me of my teen years.

When Byron called in my sister, we shook hands and he ran through everything he wanted from Michelle. Then he turned to me.

'Ben, aren't you going to audition?' he said.

'Nah,' I said. 'It's not really my thing.'

'Seriously, it'll take two minutes of your time,' he said. 'Just dance, buddy.'

'No.'

Two weeks later, I was announced on the shortlist for the role. Later, I got another call to say I hadn't made the final cut. 'I'm so sorry,' an assistant said, in a well-rehearsed tone of consolation. 'But seriously: we loved you so much this time around, we'll keep you on the books. How does that sound?' Despite myself, I was flattered. Because if I had learned anything from all my years at acting school, it was that being kept on someone's books was one of the most important things for your career. Being on the books meant that people were thinking about you. Being on the books meant you still had a chance to make it big.

Skeletons

Growing up, none of us kids had our own wardrobe or closet. Some might interpret that as a sign of rank, Dickensian poverty – *Is it because you didn't have clothes, either?* – but it wasn't anything like that. Candy had a modest set of drawers, while Andrew, Tammy and I shared a storage closet in the hallway, each laying claim to a single shelf. Any items of clothing that needed to be hung – school uniforms, blazers, coats – were simply strung from hooks or knobs around the house in ad-hoc fashion. By the time Michelle was born, we were reaching capacity, so her garments were piled in a corner, the way a homeless person's might be, except Michelle's clothes were folded and sorted; that was the difference.

Ironically, one of the original selling points of our house had been its storage space. When my parents had first inspected it in the early '80s, their eyes had widened to take in the luxuriousness of the new, solid-brick display fortress. Compared to their last home – an unventilated apartment above a Chinese restaurant, rife with feral cats – this place was too good to be true. There was a handsome garage, a new dishwasher, two tiled bathrooms, cane furniture, and rooms so large you could almost have divided the house into wings. *Wings.* All that room.

If you wanted to be technical about it, then yes: each room did have a closet. But in all the years I lived there, these were never properly opened. There was an ancient, unspoken rule that the closets weren't ours to use. Most of the time, I forgot they were there. In our shared, cramped room, Andrew pushed our beds right up against the closet doors as though they didn't exist, as if they were walls that just happened to have knobs attached.

On rare occasions, the doors would eerily open of their own accord, like something sentient was inside and trying to get out. When that happened, Andrew and I would look into them and find solid, looming stacks of the unfamiliar: clothes we'd never worn, toys we'd never played with, stacked so haphazardly that it seemed they would topple over any second. Everything was jammed together, *just so*, achieving a weird static equilibrium, like they were sealed in gelatine.

These mysterious Babel-like piles of crap seemed to have been crammed into the wardrobes hurriedly; the word *abandoned* came to mind. But that couldn't have been the case. Our parents had bought the house new, which meant there'd been no previous occupants. So where had this stuff come from?

*

For years, I'd grown up with the vaguest knowledge that in 1986 – when I was four years old – the Federal Police had raided my childhood home. It sounded exciting to me, as though I had the blood of bandits and outlaws running through my veins. The police had been looking for my aunties and uncles – my mother's siblings – who'd been staying in Australia illegally. On the rare occasions this was mentioned, I pictured raids with guns, batons and flashlights, my frightened, crying young Chinese cousins hidden in the closets like Elian Gonzalez.

But none of my siblings or cousins in Australia remembered the exact details. Everyone was too young.

The story began in the late 1970s, a time when the population of Hong Kong was reduced to mute terror at the prospect of their region being taken over by the Chinese government. My mother had moved to Hong Kong from Malaysia years earlier, as a fifteen-year-old, after her family heard reports that ethnic Malays were murdering Chinese people. Now, in Hong Kong, those who'd seen the Chinese regime in action on the mainland had come back with their own horror stories: children forced to beat their parents, food contaminated by human faeces, people resorting to cannibalism. The British and the Chinese governments were starting to bicker about the terms and conditions of the proposed handover in 1997. For Hong Kong citizens, it was like watching two dysfunctional parents fight for their custody, and suspecting your abusive father was going to win out.

'You didn't wait until 1997,' Mum explained. 'You left straightaway. What if the Chinese stamped your documents, never allowing you to leave Hong Kong again? As if Hong Kong people weren't *scared*! They were scared to *death*. You'd shit yourself. If they didn't kill you, they'd torture you slowly, using your own family: your own flesh and blood! Hitler? He'd gas you, killing you instantly in private. The Communists? They'd torture you slowly and in public.'

For her siblings, any place would do: America, Canada, England. But the obvious pick was Australia, where their two youngest sisters – my mother and aunty – had already settled. Even my aunty's husband had been granted citizenship after the Australian government announced a snap amnesty for all illegal immigrants. Who'd even heard of such a thing? Emboldened by the hope that they'd be granted similar concessions by a friendly government, my aunties and uncles started drawing up travel plans. They looked at maps, read up about the wildlife, asked their sisters questions, studied travel guides.

By the time I was born, strange things started arriving in my parents' mail. Cartons of books, boxes of socks, all heralding the imminent arrival of their Hong Kong owners. An avalanche of people followed. Over three years, a total of sixteen members of my mother's extended family – men, women, children – trickled into the country on tourist visas, ready for a new start. The men were handsomely moustached; the women looked like exotic Shanghai models; the bug-eyed children were puppy-dog cute. With every batch of arrivals at the airport, the relatives hugged each other so tightly from relief and joy that it felt like they might suffocate each other.

After a few months in the country, it wasn't long before they started doing distinctly un-tourist-like things: setting up businesses, investing in property, getting pregnant, renting homes, sending their kids to the local school. They let their visas expire, quietly and without ceremony. The family pooled their resources and started a Chinese restaurant, which became an immediate and roaring success. Everyone knew my family by name. For a business packed with illegal immigrants, it was a surprisingly slick and public enterprise, operating in the open and without shame. Life was good.

For the first time in years, my mother was happy. In the first few years of her marriage, she'd felt isolated and cut off from her family; now everyone was a thirty-minute drive away. That year, she'd also gotten pregnant again. After two boys, she had a feeling it might be another girl. Coincidentally, her older sister,

Janette, the other Australian citizen, was pregnant too, as was their sister-in-law Estelle. All the women in the family cooed. 'Wouldn't it be funny,' they asked, 'if you had your babies at the same time?' The men of the family were more crass. 'Wouldn't it be funny,' they asked, 'if we found out your husbands liked to have sex at the same time?' Everyone shrieked and made hooting noises. In amongst all the laughs was another simple question. But to say it out loud would have jinxed things, so no one did. *What was the worst that could possibly happen?*

*

All it takes is a phone call to change everything. It was night-time when Dad phoned Mum from work. Candy and Andrew were already asleep, while I was watching television and drinking milk, an oblivious four-year-old blob on the carpet.

'Don't be scared,' Dad told Mum. 'But I'm going to tell you something serious, and I don't want you to panic. Just stay calm, and listen to me carefully.'

The Federal Police, he told her, had just raided her brothers' restaurant. They'd taken her two older brothers, but had left the women and children behind. Her younger brother, Justin, had tried to escape, and no one knew where he was. 'In a few minutes,' my father told her, 'police will come knocking on our door too.'

Mum didn't have time to panic: as soon as she hung up the receiver, the doorbell rang. Two white men in suits showed her their badges. They were from the AFP.

'We need to search your house.'

As the two men entered and began to question her, she instinctively put her hands on her pregnant belly.

'Do you know your siblings are living here illegally, and on expired visas?' asked one of the men.

'Do you know where your youngest brother is at this very moment?' asked the other.

She said she didn't, and it was true. As they searched our house, Mum was afraid they'd wake Candy and Andrew. 'These are your kids?' the officers asked. They kept sleeping. By this point, she didn't know how to react. Are you meant to look shocked? Are you meant to look sad? How do you put the Federal Police off your entire family's scent? Or would that make you a criminal too? When they had finished searching, they thanked Mum, gave her their contact details and left. As soon as she heard their car engine start, she began making phone calls.

Over the next few hours, everything unravelled. Uncle Justin, Mum learned, had made a hasty escape with his pregnant wife and daughter, slipping out the back door of the restaurant and speeding down the highway.

'Go, go, go!' he'd said to his wife Aunty Estelle, ushering her into the car. '*Now.*'

By the time he was caught, they had rounded up our eldest aunty too. In the back of the police vehicles, the four Hong Kong siblings whispered in Cantonese. *Why would the police have come directly to the restaurant? How did they know exactly where to come, and at what time?* Someone had ratted on them, but who? Customers? Staff? A family member? Either way, they agreed they were in deep shit. Their journey in the police car took hours, all through the night, and led them to a remote place, the name of which would eventually become infamous. It was in a different state altogether, and was a centre called Villawood.

The next day, they were allowed some phone calls, and one of the first they made was to my mother. 'Do you even get what's happening?' our eldest aunty asked on the phone, crying. 'Do you understand how serious this is? We're basically in prison here, sister. *Prison.*'

'Don't worry, she's over-reacting,' Uncle Toby said, taking over the receiver. 'It's not all bad. You know they're feeding us steak here? Actual steak! And milk, too. Can you imagine prisoners back in Hong Kong? They'd say we were in a *hotel.*'

All of this made for front-page headlines. Over the next few months, the saga played out in the news, with more than fifty reports about the case published all around the country: the *Sunshine Coast Daily*, the *Telegraph*, *Noosa News*, the *Daily Sun* and the *Courier-Mail*. Alongside the standard headlines – *COAST FAMILY AWAITS FATE*; *DEPORTATION ORDERED FOR FAMILY*; *RESIDENCY BID REJECTED* – was the tale of my Aunty Estelle, a sweet, apple-cheeked woman and the heavily pregnant wife of Uncle Justin. She became the public face of the family's campaign. After her husband was arrested, she had gone into labour. Detained in Villawood, he hadn't yet seen his newborn child. 'I want to see my husband again,' Estelle told the newspapers in her fragile, hesitant English. 'I want them to release him so he can see me again and my baby.'

All the photographs in the newspapers were the same: the squishy-faced Chinese newborn, cradled by her distressed and blameless-looking young mother. Was this really the face of a queue-jumping threat to national security? If so, it was pretty adorable, everyone thought. And weren't Chinese babies so *cute*? The public ate it up. *BABY TIFFANY'S AN AUSSIE*, proclaimed one newspaper. *MUM MAKES TEARFUL PLEA*, said another.

But underneath the cuteness was a basic conundrum: the newest member of the family – an infant girl – was an Australian citizen, and her family wasn't.

Concerned citizens and classmates wrote editorials (*Family Here for Sake of Children*; *Visitors Pay Their Dues*; *Don't Deport Our Friends*), and petitioned the immigration minister directly. Schoolteachers mournfully displayed my cousin's white debutante dress to newspaper reporters, telling them she'd never get to wear the dress if she was sent back to Hong Kong. *Think of the children!* they howled. But for my cousins, who remained in limbo at our place, it was like an extended sleepover. Andrew and I moulded playdough with them, while Mum and her sisters-in-law fretted over meals in the kitchen. We'd make them entire tenpin bowling sets out of dough, and were disappointed and baffled when we found no one could even pretend to be interested.

They left in stages, family by family, newspaper report by newspaper report. No matter how many applications were filed, petitions sent or campaigns established, nothing was of any use. Then, only weeks after my mother's thirty-second birthday, she said goodbye to her two elderly parents at the airport. They were the last to leave, having been asked by the government to go voluntarily after their application for sponsorship was rejected. Mum was four months' pregnant by then. When they left, her parents asked what the use of crying was.

*

Everyone left their stuff behind: bags of clothes, boxes of shoes, board games and trinkets. My mother dutifully packed it all into the garage, into wardrobes, into closets – every spare inch of space she could find, assuming they'd be back one day to collect it. But when she rang them up in Hong Kong, they told her to dump it all, throw it away, treat it as garbage. 'What's the use of holding on?' they asked. 'What's happened has happened.'

As the years passed, we went on to accumulate piles of crap of our own, too, toys and clothes, books and CDs, electronics and games – the childhood detritus every suburban home acquires. Living directly opposite a major shopping centre didn't help, and we didn't have a basement or attic. We never got rid of anything: there were no spring cleans or annual audits, garage sales or visits to the tip. Instead, we were sentimental to the point where it became pathological. Even now, our school books are lodged in our backpacks – one for each year – and stowed in the garage like filed evidence. My mother's walls are adorned with my high-school artworks, including the painting *Alien Birth from a Womb of Pus* (Benjamin Law, 1998), the clay sculpture *Bird Emerges from Household Toilet Eating Snakes* (1996) and the installation work *Angel-Demon Twins Inside Papier-Maché Uterus* (1999). Mum kept everything: every book we ever read, all the tennis trophies and tenpin-bowling medals we won. Things accumulated like plaque, growing out ramshackle from the walls. As we grew, the house contracted. We found ourselves tiptoeing around piles of ancient magazines and shoeboxes of old school projects, and I became too embarrassed to have friends sleep over.

When I was a teenager and after my parents had divorced, my Uncle Toby visited us from Canada. We didn't know much about Mum's older brother, although he told us he'd once lived in Australia too. We were probably too young to remember, he said, but it was okay if we'd forgotten. Uncle Toby was charismatic and his English was good, which made us feel even more ashamed when, upon inspecting our house, he was dumbfounded. Why was our house so cluttered? No, no. 'Cluttered' was the wrong word: to his eyes, the place looked like a dump. With a stranger's eyes cast over our house, I could suddenly see it for what it was: a mess.

'This is terrible,' Uncle Toby said to my Mum in Cantonese. 'What's happened here? How can you live like this?'

The exchange made us uncomfortable, as though he was confirming something we'd suspected for a long time: there was something wrong with us. 'I'm only here for a little while,' Uncle Toby told us all. 'But at least we can try to tidy up this house while I'm here, right?'

When he said that, I felt like punching my fist in the air. *Yeah! Let's get rid of it all! Hell, let's build a goddamned FIRE.*

Throughout the week, Uncle Toby took it upon himself to take stuff to the tip, clearing out the living room and some of the garage. He wouldn't have time for our closets. The whole time, Mum hovered nearby, wringing her fingers, unsure how to intervene or contribute. Eventually, looking numb, she backed off entirely, unable to bring herself to get involved.

'Do you need to keep this?' Uncle Toby would ask her in Cantonese, holding up an old book or magazine collection, old cassettes or a bag of marbles.

'I don't know,' Mum said quietly. 'I just don't know.'

'What do you mean, *you don't know?*'

Only a few days later, the living room was unrecognisable. It was clean, and you could walk in a diagonal line from one corner to the other, just like at my friends' places. *Friends*, I thought. *I could invite my friends over.* 'And look,' Uncle Toby said, leading us through our own house, as though we'd never seen it before, which, in one sense, we hadn't. 'When you open this liquor cabinet,' he said, opening the latch, 'this light inside comes on automatically! Did you know that?'

No, I didn't know that! I thought. Hell, I didn't know we had a liquor cabinet. And there it was, with actual liquor inside too! I was almost nauseous with excitement. Now we were like those families in magazines, the ones who served food on matching crockery, and who drank water from glasses instead of mismatched mugs. We applauded.

In the days after Uncle Toby flew back to Canada, Tammy and I wore thick socks and skidded across the new-found space on the tiles.

'Look, Mum!' Tammy said. 'We're ice-skating!'

But Mum remained quiet, which was odd for her. Then she burst into tears.

'Your uncle came in like a cyclone,' she said, sobbing. All sorts of things in the garage had been thrown out, she said, and now she couldn't even figure out what was missing. It was too difficult, and she was confused. 'After everything that's happened,' she said, 'he should know better.'

We had no idea what she was talking about. *What* had happened, and *why* should he know better? We didn't ask those questions then, but we sensed they had something to do with why our house had become a museum over the years, preserving artefacts from an era I didn't even begin to understand.

After Uncle Toby's cyclonic clean-up, things managed to creep back into the house. Nowadays, the house itself is falling apart too, as though all those years of being over capacity have taken their toll. Right now, my siblings and I are trying to help

Mum move out, sell off the land, demolish the house, get rid of it all. 'What's the use of holding on?' we ask her. The doorknobs of the storage closet that Andrew, Tammy and I used to share have broken off and are now attached only by masking tape and twine. Everything has been left behind, still inside the closets, with the doors sealed shut like a tomb, like a vault, or something that's supposed to be buried.

We Have the Technology

As a teenager, I developed this weird limp. Whenever I had a medical problem – and there were many by this stage – my mother would take me to see Doctor Mark, the handsome young Irish doctor down the road, whose boyish good looks I found both attractive and intimidating. Thanks to his Aryan bone structure and Hollywood teeth, telling Doctor Mark about my bad skin, anxiety attacks and back pain – all while wearing a food-encrusted orthodontic plate – was humiliating and made me feel repulsive. But I figured there was no other option.

'What seems to be the problem?' Doctor Mark asked.

Mum nodded to cue me, so I started to mumble about my limp: a crazy peg-legged walk that had only developed in the last six months. Walking used to be an automatic task that didn't require any thought, but now it was a gruelling, self-conscious ordeal just to get from my locker to the tuckshop. As I hobbled through the school quadrangle, I could feel my brain straining to move my legs. Jocks with names like Adam and Jonathan would yell out and laugh at me. I kept my head down to avoid making eye contact, which meant I had a bird's eye view of how weird my stride had become; it was the drunken waltz of a demented pirate. After a day of limping like this, my back would be sore, my knees inflamed. This limp was ruining my life, but I didn't tell Doctor Mark that.

'I have a limp,' I said.

Doctor Mark nodded as I answered his questions. 'Well, I'll need to see this for myself,' he said, rolling up his sleeves. There wasn't enough space to walk up and down in his office, so the three of us went outside to the carpark, and Doctor Mark told me to parade for him in the disabled zone. As I walked back and forth in a staggered rhythm, Doctor Mark and Mum observed me, concerned, whispering questions to each other. *How long has he been walking like this? Is this normal, doctor?* Cars pulled up and passengers watched the display encouragingly, rallying for this young Chinese amputee who was clearly giving his new prosthesis a test run.

When we sat back down in his office, the news was grim.

'What you have,' Doctor Mark said, 'is a disease.' He explained that my condition was a result of the muscles and bones in my leg growing at different rates. This was apparently common in adolescent boys experiencing growth spurts and, in most cases, eventually sorted itself out. On one hand, I should have felt better hearing all this; it didn't sound especially serious. On the other hand, I was diseased. As I took in the news, I slouched in my chair. Mum scowled at me and gave Doctor Mark a pleading look.

'You know, Ben,' Doctor Mark said, grinning at Mum. 'You can always make these things worse with a bad posture.' At that, I immediately straightened up; not so much for my back's sake, but because I wanted Doctor Mark to like me.

As soon as we got home, I sat down at the computer and immediately started slouching again. My mother bristled. 'You know what's ruined your back?' she said. 'It's not just that limp. It's all that *slouching*. You're always sitting in front of your *boxes* and slouching.' By 'boxes,' Mum meant the various oblong obsessions that had apparently corrupted me over the years. There were magazines and novels to begin with, and then the Walkmans, video games, televisions and computers that had infiltrated my life, reducing to an empty shell the child she had raised and loved. 'See, you're even slouching now,' she said. 'And you don't even notice it. Also, you *never* talk to me anymore. You're always talking to that *box.*'

If the computer was ruining my back, she said, then my Walkman would ruin my hearing – although we both acknowledged that I did have weirdly excessive ear-wax, which Doctor Mark drained at least once a year, which probably affected my hearing. The Walkman was a recent purchase, a state-of-the-art Sony model with a mega-bass function. I kept it on at all hours, even at bedtime, when I'd lie in bed and listen to the Austereo broadcast of *Doctor Feelgood*, a late-night sex-advice program. Doctor Feelgood – whose real name was, incredibly, Sally Cockburn – was frank and unflinching. Women would phone in about their yeast infections, and married truckies called in with disturbing tales of having sex with other men in roadside toilets. In the morning, I'd wake up, curled around my Walkman, my back cracking, sore and twisted.

'You see,' Mum would say, watching me hobble into the bathroom, my headphones still plugged in. 'You're doing this to yourself.'

'That's not true,' I said. 'Don't you remember what Doctor Mark said? I'm *diseased.*'

As I brushed my teeth and listened to my Walkman, I realised that Mum simply didn't understand the joys of technology. She came from a different era entirely, and from a Malaysian town where they sent telegrams via monkeys; where she came from, feral dogs and homeless children delivered the mail. Hers was a generation that had embraced the television and the telephone and seemed content to leave it at that. In a way, I felt sorry for her.

*

Years later, when all the children had left home, Mum was left on her own in a house full of technology she didn't know how to use. Old computer hard-drives were stacked up in the study, beige metal slabs useful to her only as paperweights. We feared she would go crazy with loneliness and tried implementing a telephone roster. Each of us would speak to her once a week – five children, one for each weekday – by phone, the only piece of technology with which she was comfortable. Eventually, though, we became lazy. Mum would fall out of the loop, missing out on emails about our lives, and would only find out about our plans at the very last minute.

'Why does everyone "email" nowadays?' she said. 'Or this SMS. No one has time to pick up the phone and call their mother? One day, you'll think to yourself: "Oh, maybe I should call Mum! On the telephone like a normal person!" But hello! Jenny is *dead*! Yes! You will have a dead mother. Then how will you feel? Not even knowing your own mother is dead! You will feel so awful, I cannot even imagine. You will *vomit* from guilt. My dead body will stink up the house. That is how dead I will be. *Stinky dead*, because no one calls Mummy.'

We took this as our cue to introduce her to the world of mobile phones, and bought her a simple prepaid Nokia that was cheap to run and easy to use. We were all on the same network, so she could call us for free and vice versa. To our surprise, she took to the new technology easily. 'Oh, this is all you have to do to make an SMS?' she said, punching in numbers that magically became letters. 'Even someone with *brain damage* could use this.'

And so, while media commentators discussed the death of the English language at the hands of text-messaging youth, my mother's communication became more creative and avant-garde. Her texts were laced with flurries of capital letters, improvised messes of punctuation, and obsolete German characters like ß. On our birthdays, we would get SMSes recounting our births – *'All my discomfort ööö … And painful memories ÖÖÖ'* – the umlauted Os like a line of female mouths screaming in labour. She once sent me an outburst about an unhelpful shop assistant: *'Yeap! HE is a very STINgkyt stupid Cunt! L l l,MUM.'*

The Ls were her sign-off. They stood for 'love.'

*

The internet was trickier. It had been decades since my mother had used a typewriter, and it took a long time for her to understand the difference between Shift and Caps Lock.

'And this,' I said, guiding her hand, 'is a mouse.'

'Mouse?' she said. She let go of it, then took notes in her exercise book, drawing a cartoon mouse with the Chinese character for 'mouse' on top. 'Oh, I see,' she said. 'Because it has a *tail*! Hello, *mousey*!'

She started petting it, then drew a tail in the notebook.

'Stop that,' I said. 'You're getting distracted.'

'You don't understand! If I don't write it down, I'll never *learn*!'

'When you're writing stuff down, you're not looking at the *screen*.'

I showed her how the mouse controlled an arrow on the screen.

'And why do I want this "arrow"?' she asked. 'What does this arrow do, exactly?'

'Well,' I said, 'it points to things.'

Many computer concepts, I soon realised, were pretty abstract. When we checked her email, she would ask confounding questions, Sphinx-like riddles that melted my brain. What *was* the internet? Was Google a part of the internet? What was the difference between Facebook and Google? Was Facebook controlled by the mouse? Does everyone on Facebook use the same mouse? What was the difference between sending an email and being online? Was she online *now*? As someone who used these technologies every day, I didn't know how to answer these questions.

'So I just *goo-goo* this?' she asked, when we loaded Google. *Goo-goo*, we both knew, was a crude and childish Cantonese term for penis.

'Yes, Mum, very funny.'

'*Goo-goo*,' she said again, laughing.

Then, after a while, as we read through her emails, Mum began to slouch.

'You're slouching,' I said. 'This is why you have back pain – you slouch.'

At that, she stretched out and started singing.

'Well, I'm bored now. I'm not in the mood.' She brightened up. 'I'm going to boil an egg!'

In the kitchen, as she started boiling eggs, she asked me to print out all her emails – every single one.

'But they're already in your computer,' I said.

'Well, I can't *read* them on the computer now, can I?'

I went back to the computer and sat down. Now it was my turn to slouch.

*

Every time I go home to visit Mum, I try to incorporate a computer lesson. We seem to be making modest progress. She might not have time to compose emails herself, but she reads all the news we send her, and I'd like to think she now feels more included in our lives. Miraculously, she now prefers SMSes to phone calls for simple messages. The next step is to have her use Skype for face-to-face video chats.

During one session, I tried to show her how simple it was to video-chat with my sister Tammy, who was 100 kilometres away. Mum took careful notes the whole time I was setting up and, once we were online, took photos of the monitor, telling Tammy to smile. When we started to experience some audio feedback, I strapped a pair of headphones on her.

'Don't these things make you go deaf?' she asked. 'I remember what your Walkman did to you. Now it's that iPod.'

'I'm pretty sure you'll survive,' I said.

After about a minute with the headphones, she became flustered. 'My ears are hot,' she said to Tammy, before turning to me. 'It feels like something bit them, like some *insect*. Are your ears hot? Mine are *very hot*.' Then she started rubbing her lower back.

At precisely 4.30 p.m., Mum terminated the chat session. *The Bold & The Beautiful* was on, a show she referred to as *Staring, Staring*. ('See,' she'd explain, 'the whole episode, they just keep talking and staring at each other. *Staring, Staring*; so much staring.')

'So we're just giving up on the computer lesson, then?'

'I'm not really in the mood anymore,' she said. 'My back hurts; my ears are hot. I've been sitting down too much. And look: *Staring, Staring* is starting.'

As we sat down in front of the television, Mum leaned back against her latest purchase: an electronic massage device for her sore back, an orange latex cushion with rotating metal hands inside. When she switched it on, the hands groped out, pressing against the latex skin. It looked to me like a foetus trying to claw its way out of the womb. Hours passed. We swapped seats so I could give the massage chair a go. After we'd watched the news, two current-affairs programs and *Dancing with the Stars*, it was nearly time to go to bed. She continued to watch TV until she passed out, and I worked on my laptop until the battery died, both of us massaging our poor, atrophied muscles with the latest in domestic engineering. We hadn't done anything all day but stare at boxes.

Oceans Apart

My father doesn't believe in holidays. It's difficult to recall a time when the guy didn't work a fourteen-hour shift each day, seven days a week, fifty-two weeks a year. By New Year's Eve, he can look back and see nothing but days joined together by shifts, months threaded together by weeks, his entire waking life one giant, unending stretch of work.

It's my idea of hell. I've read that working without a break technically constitutes torture. But to my dad, the reasons why other people stop working seem strange and perhaps even lazy. He's never stopped to commemorate the birth of Jesus, the death of Jesus, the birth of the nation or the death of the Anzacs. He might sit through his own birthday with us, but it's only to humour us for an hour before he drives off to do prep in the restaurant.

Even now, he's like a machine: unstoppable, robotic, all-engines-go. What would be an unbearably relentless rhythm for normal people is his default factory-setting. After years working alongside him in his restaurants, I'd be hard-pressed to recall a time when he even went on a toilet break. It's as though he doesn't pass waste, but stores it economically somewhere on his body, to be dumped at a more convenient time. His body seems designed to operate with a cruel, business-like efficiency.

When it comes to birthdays and Christmases, what do you buy someone like that? Someone who doesn't have – or believe in – free time? You can't buy things to cater to his hobbies; he doesn't have any. Over the years, buying gifts for Dad nearly always ended in tears or in panic attacks at suburban shopping malls. He complicated things further by actively discouraging us from buying him presents, sometimes expressing his disgust so forcefully that it ruined Christmas. He's the father, he'd say. He was supposed to provide for *us*.

On Christmas Day, when it came his turn to open a present, he'd always draw out the process by meticulously cutting the sticky tape with a small dagger-like knife in monk-like silence. Once the gift was revealed, there were no expressions of delight, no thank-yous or hugs. Instead, he'd slowly scan the item with a completely neutral look on his face, turning it over in his hands like an antique dealer who knew he'd been handed a counterfeit. Eventually he'd find what he'd been looking for.

'See this?' he'd say. He'd point to a microscopic label on the side, showing it to us like a warning. *'Made in China.* No good.'

Whoever had given him the present would look devastated, and the rest of us would start to argue. 'That's not fair,' we'd say. *'You're* made in China.' It never made any difference. We were stupid to have wasted money on him like this, and he'd ask us to immediately retrieve the receipt so we could claim back the cash and buy something for ourselves – something practical, like a leather watch or an Akubra hat; something made in Australia. These suggestions always had the same effect: we'd run to our rooms, howling and slamming our doors.

I began to compile lists of potential gifts for him in advance, presents that could potentially, conceivably work: olive-leaf extract as a health tonic; a wind-up torch for emergencies; paw-paw ointment for burns inflicted at the restaurant. Individually, these small items made sense, but I'd assemble them side by side in a makeshift 'hamper' – really a disused shoebox packed with cellophane – only to realise they looked ridiculous alongside each other, like a cobbled-together prize in a badly planned church raffle. More recently, I made another list, of all the things I knew about my father, hoping it would provide clues as to what to buy. The list depressed me:

1. Dad likes eating fruit.
2. Dad has mild diabetes.
3. Dad works a lot.
4. Dad watches Chinese soap operas.
5. Dad is losing his hair and I will too.
6. Dad reads the newspaper every day.
7. [*blank*]
8. Dad likes eating fruit.

That year, I gave up and handed over a thick ream of Instant Scratch-Its for his birthday. As much as this seemed like a legitimate birthday present, we both silently acknowledged that it was also a gesture of defeat. 'Happy birthday,' I said glumly. 'Enjoy the scratching.'

When the tables were turned and Dad had to give the kids presents, it was less of a challenge than you'd expect. Whether it was a birthday, a wedding or a marriage, a lot of Chinese parents took the same approach to gift-giving, one shared by Mafia hitmen and pirates: just hand over thick wads of cash. As a kid, I loved the tradition and pageantry of it, but that changed when I became a teenager and felt no one understood me, least of all my father. I began to regard this open slather of cash as coarse and insulting. Couldn't he put in some effort to find out what I actually liked? Cash was something you gave to employees, maids and prostitutes, not your children. If my father and I were honest with ourselves, we'd realise that gifts weren't just gifts, but a test of how well you knew a person. It was starting to feel as though we'd done nothing over the years but fail, fail, fail.

*

Bear with me while we skip back a decade or five and travel through time and space to investigate another father–son relationship, this one set in China. My dad and his own father only saw each other once in their entire lives, when Dad was around twelve. Give him any sympathy about the fact now, and he'll make a little dismissive noise.

'Come on,' Dad says. 'It's not that sad. Sure, I never saw my dad growing up, but what are you going to do? *Cry* about it?' Which is, of course, exactly what I would have done.

Just after my grandfather got my grandmother pregnant, he moved out of their small village on the outskirts of Canton to work in San Francisco. The contrast between the two places couldn't have been greater: one was a robust modern city undergoing a blooming post-war renaissance; the other was a village with no sanitation. Back in my grandparents' village, human shit was collected every few days by government workers and pooled as a slurry-like fertiliser for edible crops. I would have left too.

My grandfather reasoned with his wife. 'I'll be earning American dollars over there,' he said, 'so you'll never need to worry about money to raise our son.'

Over in the US, my grandfather soon found work as the head of staff at the local Mandarin Club – a sort of gentlemen's club for Chinese-speakers and Sinophiles – and would wire American dollars back to his wife and the son he'd never met. Back in China, Dad heard only the vaguest stories about his father, not enough to cement an image in his mind: his father was generous; his father worked hard; his father always thought about his family; his father was good. Those were the only things he knew.

Things in San Francisco became more dour. Lonely and guilt-ridden, my grandfather drank in the evenings after hearing stories from relatives about his wife and boy back home. 'Back in China,' they'd tell him, 'your kid's as skinny as a rake. What are they eating down there? Tumbleweeds? Thistles?' My Dad was just a runt of a kid and there wasn't any problem, but comments like these were enough to make a father fret.

When Dad and his mum moved to Hong Kong, my grand-father started doing some depressing calculations. A one-way trip from San Francisco to Hong Kong would take weeks by boat, and a tonne of savings. Once he got there, he'd have to stay and not look back to make it worth the time and money. But this wasn't his main worry: the idea of meeting his son for the first time terrified him. How do you say hello to a son you've never met? He thought he'd like to get him something for the occasion – a stuffed animal, a toy – but would he be too old for that sort of thing now? What animals did he like, anyway? *Would he even know who he was?* Stewing over these questions kept him up at night, and he'd go to work the next day feeling ragged. After work every night, he'd drink, wire more money to my grand-mother, douse the night with whisky and fumigate his head with cigar smoke, until he finally passed out.

*

To sail from San Francisco to Hong Kong takes roughly a month. Look at a world map, and you'll see the space between the two points is a massive expanse of blue – one of the largest stretches of water on the globe – with hardly any land to interrupt the endlessness of it all. There's just water – lots of water. If you're lucky, you might pass a Hawaiian island, but of all the cross-oceanic journeys you can take, it's perhaps the most boring. Every waking day looks exactly like the last, and you begin to question whether the ship is moving at all. And you have a lot of time to think. On those nights sailing from America to Asia, my grandfather would have insomnia and would drink whisky to lull himself into unconsciousness, leaving him feeling more anxious and seasick the next morning.

When he arrived at the Hong Kong apartment where his son and wife lived, he took a moment outside the door before knocking. He was sweating a lot, had been nursing a headache all day, and the long ocean voyage had disoriented the hell out of him. With a sinking feeling, he realised he'd forgotten to buy his kid a present. *Why hadn't he bought anything?* But before he could knock, the doors flew open and a cacophony of voices took over.

'You're here, you're here—'

'Come inside, yes!'

'Take *off* that coat! Such a *beautiful* coat but it's so *hot*—'

'The journey by boat must have taken you *so* long! To think—'

'Don't be silly, take a seat, take a *seat*!'

Hands were everywhere, faces smashed into his, and he didn't know where to look. In front of him was the wife he hadn't seen in a decade. Over there: his sister-in-law and whip-smart niece. And in the middle of them all was a shy, pigeon-toed twelve-year-old, scrawny as hell with a head like a bobble.

'Well, look at you,' he said to his son. *'Ah Leung.* Do you know who I am?'

'Hello, *Ba-Ba,*' his son replied quietly. 'I'm pleased to meet you after all this time.'

My grandfather laughed at the politeness of his kid, and everyone else joined in. 'My son,' he said. 'What a nice guy!' Even though he was a little overweight, he leaned over and picked up his son effortlessly, gave him a squeeze and marvelled at how light he was – almost like a sack of hollow bones.

Is it possible to describe what happened next without sounding like a liar? Because what took place after this is the stuff of the strangest fiction, a plot contrivance so unrealistic it would seem manipulative to include it, if it hadn't actually happened. But it did happen: thirty minutes later, my grandfather was dead. One moment he was chatting and bouncing my father on his knee; the next he was putting his hands to his forehead, saying a polite 'Excuse me,' before collapsing on the floor, sprawled across the apartment tiles.

The women started screaming and flocked around him, bouncing from foot to foot and wringing their hands.

'What's happening, what's *happening*?'

One of the men checked for a pulse – *'Call an ambulance!'* – while another relative slapped him in the face, calling out his name.

'Can you hear me? *CAN YOU HEAR ME?*'

My bug-eyed dad, just a kid, stood in the background perfectly still, his mouth forming a stunned little O.

'Okay, okay!' Dad's cousin said. 'Calm down! Ring the ambulance, yes, but help me check his goddamned pockets first!'

In emergencies, people tend to respond to clear directions, and this situation wasn't any different. Everyone helped remove my grandfather's American coat and shirt, and they went through his pockets and felt under his trousers. What they were looking for was money: traveller's cheques, cash – anything the ambulance officers might soon enough steal. On his waist they found a travel belt containing tidy stacks of cash, in both American and Hong Kong currency. His body was covered in the stuff.

Things happened quickly after that: the ambulance hauling him away to the hospital, the confirmation of death, the weird funeral days later, everyone more confused than mournful, melancholy rather than sad, the way people are when they bury someone they haven't seen in over a decade. Afterwards, the family used the money. They put half of it into the bank, invested the rest in enough apartments to house seven tenants, and started collecting rent. In the end, my grandfather had been right about working in San Francisco. His family would never have to worry about money.

'He came back, and I think he was too happy,' Dad says now. 'Maybe over-happy. It was like his brain – it was bleeding.' He wasn't drunk when they met, Dad clarifies. He was just over-excited. Sometimes, he says, you just get so excited your head explodes, you know? *Ka-boom*: just like that.

*

After years of searching for gifts suitable for Dad, I think I've made a breakthrough. Ever since he and my mother divorced, the signs have been there. There is a universal image associated with single fathers the world over: decaying Y-fronts hanging on the line, handwashed in substances other than laundry detergent. (In Dad's case, that substance was Dettol.) His underpants looked as though a plague of locusts had devoured them. The material was so threadbare that to use it as a rag – which he eventually did – seemed an insult; an insult to rags.

Still, buying underwear was difficult. Every pair of jocks or panties, no matter what the brand, originates from China. You can have as many merino sheep, kangaroos, Akubra hats, Australian flags or Pat Rafters on the packaging as you like, but the fact remains: those garments come from the vast, mystic land of the Orient. They're not made by hardened sheep farmers and their weather-beaten wives, but by Chinese women and children who don't know who Pat Rafter is and have no need for hats because they work and sleep in factories, where they debate whether the giant hopping rat on the label would be any good for food. In the end, I resorted to mail-order briefs.

On his sixtieth birthday, when he opened the ethically produced, organically grown, sustainably managed American underwear I had bought him online, something strange happened. He smiled, and even commented on the bright colours I'd chosen: pine-forest green, bruised-face purple, baby-turd mustard. For a moment, I thought we were going to have a genuine father–son moment. But instead he leapt up, instructing us all to wait while he got something from his bedroom-office. When he returned, he was carrying five red envelopes, one for each child, each with a thick wad of cash inside. We started protesting. What was he doing, giving us money? It was his birthday, not ours.

'But it's a special occasion, isn't it?' he said. 'And you bought me presents, so these are presents for you!'

THE FAMILY LAW

We tried to explain that wasn't how it worked, but he looked so happy – it felt mean-spirited to argue with him. 'Thanks, Dad,' we said in unison, and we kissed him. Then Dad dusted his hands and announced he needed to go to work. As usual, no cake, no ceremony – no need.

We drove away from Dad's place in silence, until finally someone spoke.

'Sometimes I get the feeling Dad doesn't understand the concept of presents.'

'Yeah,' Michelle said. 'Why did Dad give us money? It's *his* birthday.'

'Every time he does something like this,' Tammy added, 'I feel weird and guilty.'

As we drove on in silence, I started compiling a new list in my mind. This one was of all my preconceptions about work and family. I'd always thought of absent parents as negligent, but perhaps for some parents, working so hard that you never saw your family was a weird sign of love. Maybe knowing nothing about your children could be a strange sign of affection. Or maybe not. After we parked the car, we tore open our red envelopes and started counting the money inside, comparing notes on what we'd buy with it from the shopping centre: clothes and kitchen appliances; gadgets and homewares – all of them probably made in China.

Amongst the Living Dead

For as long as I can remember, I've thought about my mother's death on a daily basis. This wouldn't be such a strange exercise if she were actually dead, but the thing is, my mother's alive – perhaps aggressively so. For her entire life, her good health has defied a lifestyle both lacking in exercise and revolving around dietary habits like eating butter in quantities usually associated with cheese. She's got the heart of an ox and the skin of a cosmetics model; she's a woman in her fifties who still gets checked for ID. Still, despite her rude health, some strange force has always compelled her to remind her children of her imminent death.

'Mum,' you might say, 'I need some space.'

'Well, you'll have all the space you need,' she'll say, 'when I'm *dead*.'

Or: 'Mum, I'm not going to buy this today – I can't afford it.'

'Buy it,' she'll say. 'You'll have all the money you need – when I'm *dead*.'

She sees her own death everywhere: a loose showerhead, a shoe without grip, an unlocked car door, a taxi driver with a weird look about him. These macabre what-if scenarios aren't limited to her own fate. In her eyes, death looms over us too, and we were taught to see it everywhere. As kids, Mum would pull us to her chest tightly every time we crossed the road for milk (we could get mowed down by a truck), or squeeze us close before we drove off to swimming lessons (all it takes is a shallow bath for a child to drown). When one of us would leave for school camp, she'd weep openly after our departure like a Mediterranean widow, because she knew – just knew – we'd be coming home in a body bag, having been torn limb from limb by a wild, rabies-infected beast thirsty for child-blood. It made for anxious formative years, and made us repeat the same question in our minds, over and over again: *Do you know something we don't?*

Maybe she did. She'd experienced deaths in her own family, and we hadn't. And because Mum watched the news voraciously, she'd come to the grim conclusion that the Sunshine Coast was the nation's capital for missing and dead children. Even now, there's something about the region's terrain, its combination of coastline, mountains, hinterland and bush, that seems conducive to unseen phantoms, killers and boogiemen on the prowl for kids. The most notorious case took place when I was five, when a twelve-year-old schoolgirl called Sian – a friend of my cousin's – was abducted, raped, tortured and murdered by a psychotic married couple obsessed with virgins. Despite being so young, I remember the case vividly, and one chilling detail has always stood out in my mind: that they pulled out the girl's fingernails before they killed her. There were also the cases of the Kenilworth babysitter killer, the lesbian vampire killers and poor Daniel Morcombe, a kid abducted while waiting for a bus – he was going to buy Christmas presents – and never seen again. In the months that followed, houses throughout the state left their front lights on for Daniel as a gesture of sympathy to the grieving family. Where we grew up, awful things happened – still happen – to children, all the time.

*

There were two times in particular when Mum was convinced I was dead. Both involved my brother Andrew, and occurred before the advent of mobile phones.

Our school, a large campus, had been built in the middle of a rainforest, a shortsighted man-made intrusion into nature's promiscuous growth. The place was like a jungle; the rainforest would have reclaimed the school grounds in weeks if the gardeners had let it. It was as if the campus was designed to eat children: no one would ever find a lost child in there. If you were lucky, maybe the thick, tentacled forest would spit out a child-sized skeleton a few weeks later, just to give you some closure.

Both Mum and Andrew claim not to remember the first incident, but I'm sure it happened. I certainly remember the screaming afterwards. Mum had come to school for a parent–teacher interview and told us to meet her at a certain time and place after our classes had finished. Andrew and I had forgotten the designated meeting spot – *next to the car? outside the classroom?* – so we killed time by joining the after-school activity group in the basement of the sprawling campus. We didn't belong there, and Mum didn't even know it existed. We lost track of time. It was only when it became dark that we looked, panic-stricken, at a clock, and realised we were as good as dead.

The rest of the evening is a blur: my mother's murderously angry face upon finally finding us; her holding back tears as she led us back to the car; the engine starting and, with it, the screaming. She'd done laps around the campus calling for us, she said, loud enough to be heard, restrained enough not to sound insane. It would have been a difficult balance to strike. But in the car, she let fly with strangled howls, a curdled monologue of words and sobs that ceased to make any sense.

In the back seat, Andrew and I stared at our laps. Mum had been angry with us before, but this time seemed different. When she eventually calmed down, her catatonic tone of voice suggested we'd inflicted permanent damage.

'Mum, we're okay,' I said quietly. 'You worry too much.'

'You'd be *worried* too,' Mum hollered, 'if you thought someone you *loved* was … was—'

'Dead,' we said. 'Yes, Mum. We know.'

*

Years later, Andrew and I were both elected class captains and had to stay behind for an after-school meeting. Afterwards, we walked together to the car pick-up zone – a concrete slab with an arched metal rain shelter built above it – and sat there, expecting Mum. What we didn't know was that her plans had changed.

At home that afternoon, Mum had experienced something weird. Ever since she'd miscarried, she'd bled heavily every month, but this time was different, and she called her gynaecologist. There was a small window of opportunity for an appointment in the afternoon.

'I can't pick up the boys,' she told Dad by phone, as she cleaned up the bathroom with towels and toilet paper. 'It's like a *murder* scene here. I don't know what's *wrong* with me.'

'Right,' Dad said, looking over paperwork. He had been swept up all day in meetings, drafting plans for a new project with land-dealers and developers, real-estate agents and investors. His brain was reaching full capacity.

'I mean, every month is heavy, but this month is … You know what it's like? It's like someone's *stabbed* me,' she said. 'Down *there*. Stabbed me right in the—'

'Okay, okay.' Dad cut her off. 'I'll pick up the boys. What time?'

But as soon as Dad hung up, he went back to his plans and promptly forgot about the phone call.

Hours passed. Andrew used a pay phone to call home until our combined spare change ran out. Mosquitoes appeared, and I was allergic. I knew my skin would swell up in pink, flat islands of itchiness on my legs, before scabbing over in marks that, Andrew joked, resembled AIDS lesions. Over in the rainforest, birds and unseen creatures started shrieking at the sun as it began to sink, casting everything in a dark orange glow. It would be pitch black in less than half an hour.

'What do we do?' I asked. 'What if something bad has happened?'

I started whimpering, and Andrew rolled his eyes.

'What if Mum's … what if she's—'

'Don't say it,' he said.

We started to walk, staying close to the road, following the same route Mum used to fetch us every day. The plan was to intercept her if she came, wave her down if we saw her car. Instead, unfamiliar cars honked their horns at us for being so close to the bitumen, their headlights blaring into our eyes, stunning us like wildlife. My backpack started to hurt. It felt like my spine and vital organs were being crushed. It was Year 8, and I was still getting used to how heavy all the homework was.

'This is killing me,' I said.

'Stop being a baby,' Andrew said. 'We're nearly there.'

We trudged on. More mosquitoes came out, biting me everywhere, even on the palms of my hand. We made a detour to Dad's restaurant, which was closer. When he saw us, Dad turned ghostly white.

At that very moment, we later learned, Mum had arrived at the school's pick-up zone. This time, because it was dark and there was no one around, there was no need for her to strike a balance between volume and restraint. She screamed like someone had been murdered.

Days later, driving to school again, we tried to calm Mum down, but she just shook her head in frustration. 'You have no idea,' she said. 'None of you have any idea, not even your Dad. And you'll never have any idea until you're a mother yourself.' In the backseat, I rolled my eyes. *Well, that's a little melodramatic*, I thought.

*

More than a decade later, after the children had all left home, Mum was living alone for the first time in her life. By this stage, the Sunshine Coast had transformed again and was enjoying its new incarnation as the number-one retirement destination in the country. Old people from all over Australia swarmed to the region, attracted by its calm beaches and single-level shopping centres, and bought into estates built on man-made rafts of land that jutted out into canals. It wasn't just a place where children disappeared and died anymore. No. Now it was a place where old people died too, quietly in their homes and without anyone noticing.

It was my youngest sister, Michelle, who called me, out of the blue, to tell me that Mum might be dead. She didn't say those words exactly – didn't actually use the word *dead* – but we both understood the subtext.

'She's not picking up either phone,' Michelle said. 'And I've been calling for hours.'

Maybe she was at the shops, I suggested. Doing some gardening. Taking a very, very long nap.

'Usually, I'd think that too. Except I called her last night, and she didn't pick up then either. Then I called this morning, and I've called over ten times since then. Nothing.'

This wasn't like Mum. Immediately, my mind went back to the day before, and the last phone call I'd had with her. During the course of the conversation, she had stated the following things:

1. We did not call her enough;
2. She resented the fact we did not call her enough;
3. No one returned her calls any more and she may as well be dead; and
4. If she were to die, how would anyone know?

'I don't like this email all the time,' she said. 'Mummy wants to hear your *voices*. You can't hear your voices over the SMS.'

This went on for about half an hour. It wasn't exactly a pleasant conversation, and so, ironically, it didn't provide much incentive to stay on the line. Later I'd recognise that these outbursts came from a place of loneliness, but at the time the phone call struck me as an exercise in self-sabotage and passive aggression. It was infuriatingly brilliant: she'd phoned to complain that no one wanted to speak to her, knowing she'd aggravate me to the point where I'd cut the phone call short, all ultimately proving her point: that no one wanted to speak to her. *Well played, Jenny*, I'd thought. *Well played*.

Recalling the conversation now, I started to sweat. Usually when I sweat, I don't smell much different from normal, but if I become nervous or frightened, my armpits begin to smell weirdly pungent and foul. From a biological perspective, I'd say it's a defence mechanism similar to a skunk's. If someone were to attack me in a dark alleyway, I would smell this way. Right now, it was defending me against accusations of murder. *What if I were dead?* Mum had asked, and I realised this was the first time I'd really heard the question, processed it, and understood its implications.

We called Candy, the only sibling who lived within a twenty-kilometre radius of Mum. Again, we avoided the word 'dead,' and instead asked her to check that Mum was 'okay' – which, by extension, implied 'alive.' Of all the siblings, Candy had the most fraught relationship with Mum, but she didn't hesitate for a second.

'I'll do it,' she said. 'But I don't have the keys. You'll have to tell me where the emergency ones are.'

I tried calling Mum again – on the landline, on the mobile – knowing it was futile. It didn't matter: I started to leave messages on her answering machines. *Hello!* Mum's voice said in her sing-song girly tone, the one she adopted when she spoke English to strangers. *This is Jenny! Please leave a message and I call you BACK! Have a nice day. BYE!* The staticky greeting made Mum sound like she was caught in a blizzard a thousand miles away, at the ends of the earth, some place where satellite reception was fading fast. I left messages – *Where are you? Are you dead? Why do you even have a phone if you're not going to leave it on?* – and kept calling and calling and calling, the same way someone continues with CPR, long after they know the person is beyond resuscitation.

'She's not here,' Candy said when she called back. 'No one's home.'

That's when I started calling the hospitals, started thinking awful things. *She's slipped in the shower. She's electrocuted herself. She choked on something simple – a piece of fruit, a raw nut, something I could have knocked out of her in a second and now she's … she's—*

All of the people on the hospital phone lines said the same ominous thing before transferring me to another line: 'You'll want the emergency ward then.' But when I got through to the ERs, they all told me no one had been admitted under our mother's name, but that things like this happened all the time, and that I really shouldn't worry, because they were sure she'd be fine.

We couldn't do anything but wait, our phones in our hands. How could we know that she'd done all of this on purpose, to see whether her children cared enough? All we could do was prepare for the worst and hope for the best, trying to make our cries loud enough to be heard but restrained enough not to seem insane.

In the Mood

Singing in the choir was mandatory at my primary school. Every few months we would be marched past the oval, down the terraces and into the nursing home run by the local church. We would line up at the door in two single-file lines – one of boys, one of girls – bracing ourselves to be hit by a wall of odour: bleach, mothballs, powdered soup, a slight hint of faeces. When the doors opened, the sheer force of the smell would knock everyone backwards, making it difficult to breathe.

'*Whoa*,' the boys said, putting up their hands.

'Don't be *mean*,' the girls hissed back. 'They can't help it.'

By *they*, the girls meant the forty or so senior citizens who'd been rounded up to watch us perform. When we were finally assembled in their common room to sing, our voices would be strained; it was difficult to hold a melody without inhaling. We'd start off with hymns, then follow up with 'In the Mood,' a bouncy big-band number that called for dancing and movement. Considering how many people were wheelchair-bound or recovering from strokes, the choice struck me as somewhat cruel.

After we finished, only a handful of people clapped. Most of the elderly residents just stared into their laps. Men in their eighties spontaneously fell asleep in the middle of our hymns, their heads rolling back at such severe angles, it looked as if they'd broken their necks. We were surprised they didn't swallow their tongues.

Years later, in high school, the art students were asked to paint a mural in the same facility for a resident with a severe disability, who was described to us as 'a danger to himself.' Part of the appeal of the task was that his room had padded walls, which sounded like something out of a Hollywood movie set in an asylum. But I was disappointed: the pads weren't marvels of medical design; instead, they were just old, single-spring mattresses pushed against the wall and held together by occy straps.

We pulled the mattresses down and painted the off-white walls with a montage of birds, trees and rainbows. After we'd been at work for a while, a nurse wheeled in the man who lived in the room.

'So this is David!' the nurse said. 'Say hello, David!'

David groaned politely and looked at the floor.

The first thing I noticed were his long toenails protruding from beneath the blanket. *Claws*, I immediately thought. *David has claws*. But despite his gnarled features and the drooling, I remember thinking that if David had been treated to a salon-style haircut, a pedicure and a pair of Italian loafers, he would've been something close to handsome. But the only leather accessories on David that day were the series of buckles that acted as restraints. 'David just wanted to tell you how much he appreciates the job you kids are doing. Doesn't this look wonderful, David? The colours are so … *bright*!'

She nudged David, and he reluctantly looked up at the walls. He scanned the mural-in-progress suspiciously with his one good eye, up and down. After a moment of silence, he started to groan. Soon he was thrashing against his buckles, but they held him in tightly. My art teacher – a pleasant British woman in overalls – straightened up in alarm and spread out her arms, as if to protect us. As David continued to moan and howl, I looked at our mural with all of its vivid, perky colours. If I were forced to look at it every day, I'd probably want to scream too, I realised. I felt bad for the guy.

'Okay!' the nurse said brightly. 'David and I just wanted to say hello!' David continued screaming as she wheeled him off.

'*Well*,' our art teacher said to us. 'Don't be rude. Say hello back.'

We all waved from a safe distance as David thrashed against his wheelchair.

'Hello,' we all said quietly.

*

When I was an adult, my mother and I visited my maternal grandmother – my *Poh-Poh* – in various nursing facilities throughout Hong Kong. Although she was shuffled around a lot over the years, I was always struck by how cramped the facilities were. Hong Kong is renowned for its lack of space, but this was something else. All the nursing homes were designed as if to accommodate shrunken orphan amputees, with tiny beds pushed alongside one another, each with a stowaway cabinet underneath, big enough to store thimbles and buttons, not all the earthly possessions you'd acquired over eighty years. Walking into these places, I suddenly understood what it must be like to be a claustrophobe.

On one of our visits, Mum and Poh-Poh started to cry together quietly on Poh-Poh's bed. I knew what they were discussing: Poh-Poh felt trapped and rejected by her six surviving children; Mum wanted to bring her back to Australia with us. But we all knew it was impossible. My grandmother had already been deported once from Australia. In any case, it would have been regarded as shameful for her to live with one of her daughters rather than a son. I hovered nearby until I couldn't stand it any longer and wandered off to give them some privacy.

Walking down the hall, past the kitchen with its vats of congee and soup, I noticed another old woman sitting by herself on her bed, doing nothing, just staring at me. She was no larger than a toddler and her features were shrunken and wrinkled, like plastic melted in an oven. She looked at me with the saddest eyes; they made me think of an animal that knows it is about to be euthanased. When she smiled weakly, I smiled back. 'How are you?' I asked her in Cantonese.

It seemed like the polite thing to do.

It was a mistake.

'What's the use of me living at all?' she wailed in Cantonese. 'What's the *point*? I was born, gave birth to children, then they dumped me here to rot and *die*. I may as well be in the *ground* right now, except Hong Kong doesn't even have enough ground to bury me in. So they'll *burn* me instead. They'll burn my *bones*.'

As she spoke, she clutched my hand and squeezed down on it like a clamp. She had a surprisingly strong grip.

'I'm just taking up space,' she continued. 'I'm useless. Useless. I'm so goddamned *useless*. I've been dumped here to die. *Why won't God let me die?*' She looked as though she was about to cry, but her face was incapable of yielding moisture, so she winced instead. It looked painful.

I had no idea what to say back, and my vocabulary in her language was limited. Instead, I patted her on the back, as I might a baby lamb in a mobile petting zoo. *Pet, pet.* It felt useless, but I didn't know what else to do. As I patted her, nurses wearing safety masks attended to their patients, and old men around us farted in their sleep. Sitting next to this shrunken, dehydrated woman, smelling the gas from the bowels of old Chinese men, listening to the muffled weeping of my mother and my grandmother from across the corridor, I prayed no one else I knew would end up in a place like this.

*

After Poh-Poh died, my mother and I flew back to Hong Kong two more times: once for her funeral, and another time to collect her ashes. When we returned home the second time, deflated and traumatised, I heard that Ma-Ma – Dad's mother and my last living grandparent – might be moving to a retirement home. Dad insisted this place would be different. Only a forty-minute drive from the centre of Brisbane, The Gardens were advertised as a pioneering experiment: the only retirement village in Australia catering specifically for the Asian elderly. It was new and modern, clean and spacious, and built to Asian sensibilities. Instead of pools (the Chinese elderly aren't big on swimming), there would be karaoke rooms; organic vegetable patches instead of rose gardens; mah-jong tables instead of chess boards. Instead of being perched by the ocean, like a Florida resort community, The Gardens' centrepiece would be a man-made lake, complete with stone bridges, ducks and a bright red Chinese pergola. It was the type of place my mother and I had fantasised about Poh-Poh living in, if only we'd been able to bring her over.

Still, the place was a hard sell. Elderly Asian people had a fundamental aversion to the idea of retirement villages. Their idea of a nursing home was the cramped kind you find in Hong Kong or Beijing, or the culturally mismatched Australian ones filled with white people playing bingo. Shipping old folks off to these places was the ultimate shame for Asians, a last kick in the guts before your children unceremoniously rolled you, still breathing, into a shallow grave. Chinese culture dictated that an elderly mother lived with her eldest son until she died, or until the son couldn't stand it any longer and murdered her, whichever came first.

But the Gardens made everyone reconsider their prejudices, including me. On the open day, we watched adult sons and daughters shove prospectuses and price lists under the noses of their parents. 'See, Poh-Poh?' they said. 'Look, Goong-Goong! This place is different. The nurses speak the language! They serve rice every day! No one does aqua-aerobics here! You'll never have to wear a bathing suit again!' I was won over by the fact that nothing smelt like human waste, and at no stage did I see a mattress pushed up against the wall.

Dad spared no expense and moved Ma-Ma into one of the deluxe homes. Nestled in a private, quiet bend of road, these self-contained houses faced away from the main respite centre. Residents could convince themselves that they didn't live in a retirement village at all, but just happened to find themselves in a cul-de-sac alongside like-minded, elderly Asian people. A few weeks after her arrival, we knew Ma-Ma was finally at home when she'd planted vegetables, herbs and a bush of *chow sie gau*, a fragrant plant used in soups. Its name translates literally as 'reeking shit dog,' and the stuff smells like a cross between marijuana and an animal corpse. For Ma-Ma, it was the smell of home.

Still, it was a lonely existence. We all tried to visit regularly, synching our schedules, catching buses, car-pooling. On the nights we came for dinner, she'd serve herb soups – watery broths that took hours to stew – and cook massive meals no one could finish. We'd share food, laugh at stupid jokes and read magazines, until we ran out of things to say and the conversation reverted to English.

Most of the time, she was content to see us go at the end of the evening. But sometimes she'd protest. 'Why don't any of you sleep over?' she'd ask, pointing to the untouched spare room. 'I've got that bed just sitting here doing nothing. There's enough room for three of you in that thing.' At this, we'd look at each other uncomfortably and mumble our way to the car.

It always made me sad, driving away and watching her wave us off, before we headed off to our own homes. Although we were a family of eight – five kids, two parents and a grandmother – we'd splintered apart, each of us retreating into private places built for one. Some of us lived with friends or partners, but none of us lived with each other anymore. There were eight homes between us. If we wanted, we could hole up in our separate flats and houses without seeing one another for weeks – which, for my family, was a strange new experience.

*

Eventually, I decided to live with Ma-Ma for a week. Tammy had done it for a month before going overseas, and I admired her tenacity. She had survived life without an internet connection, completely surrounded by old people who clutched at her youth and cornered her for conversation. If she'd managed a month, surely I could handle seven days.

On the morning I arrived, Ma-Ma was on the phone, and the conversation looked sombre. I waved hello and hauled in box upon box of VHS tapes from the car, Hong Kong television serials I'd picked up from the local Vietnamese grocer on the way over, which had weighed down the car like a dead body. When I put down the final box of tapes, Ma-Ma hung up the phone and looked away. 'Who was on the phone?' I asked.

Ma-Ma sighed and started talking in Cantonese. 'Last week,' she said, '[—] had a fall and then she [———]. Her family is so [——]. But the [—] was too [———], and now she's [—]. Which is [———]. So very, very [———]. It just makes me want to [———]. Anyway, [————]. Don't you think? It's happening tomorrow, so I'll be [——], if that's okay with you.'

I was nodding on the outside, but inside I was alarmed. Every second word she said was a blank. I'd always prided myself on being able to understand what my grandmother said to me, but now I realised there'd usually been translators between us: my father, my mother, one of my siblings. It dawned on me that this was the first time we'd ever been alone, just the two of us, and that maybe this idea hadn't been properly thought through.

Later, my mother rang to see how we were getting along. She spoke to my grandmother first, before passing the phone to me.

'Isn't it sad how Ma-Ma's friend died?' Mum said.

'*What*? She *died*?'

Mum let out a little noise of confusion. 'Ma-Ma said she told you all about it. She had a fall, and now she's dead. Gone. At least she's with her husband now. Poor things.'

After I'd hung up the phone, I looked at my grandmother. I knew the words for when someone had died, and didn't understand how I'd missed this.

'Ma-Ma?' I said in basic Cantonese. 'I didn't know she was *dead.*'

Ma-Ma's spine stiffened a little, and I immediately realised my mistake. She had side-stepped the word *dead*, talking in euphemisms to soften the blow. In English, people *pass away*. They *go to a better place*. In Cantonese, when people die, they clearly [——] and [——]. I felt rude. No one talks about death directly – especially not in places like retirement homes. Why talk about it when you're surrounded by it? My grandmother told me I shouldn't go to the funeral. I didn't know the woman that well. Plus, my grandmother added, I really needed a haircut.

We took the next few days easy. She played mah-jong with the other residents. We went for walks when the sun went down and kicked the cane toads that terrorised the place at night. We spent our evenings watching the Hong Kong drama *Hoong Wong Sae Choong Tai*, or *Maiden's Vow*. The narrative was confusing and disorientating, with cuts between the 1900s, 1950s and today.

'Is that her sister?' I asked, pointing at the screen.

'No,' Ma-Ma said. 'She works for her.'

'And who's *he*? Is that her father?'

'No, that's the matchmaker.'

Maiden's Vow was an ambitious, multi-linear drama, following a single family across the centuries, from feudal China to contemporary Hong Kong. Narrative-wise, it was a mess, and I got sleepy trying to keep up with it. Eventually, I fished out a different DVD, something I'd stolen from my boyfriend's collection. It was *In the Mood for Love*, the one Hong Kong movie we owned. Every time I'd tried to watch it before, I had fallen asleep. My sister Candy, too, had found the slow-burning romance tedious.

'All they did was *stare* at each other,' she said. 'You wanted to scream at them, "Just take your clothes off and *fuck* already. You're wasting time with all this slow-motion walking and staring!"'

Still, I told my grandmother it was one of the few Chinese movies white people liked.

'White people watch Chinese films?' She was sceptical.

But as we watched the movie together, we both laughed in the right places. Neither of us could take our eyes off Maggie Cheung, and when she wept, we almost cried too. Her life was dramatic and tragic, and made all the more poignant by her smoking-hot beauty. I wanted to look like Tony Leung, or dress like Tony Leung, or graft Tony Leung's cheekbones into my face. For the first time, I didn't fall asleep watching it. In fact, I adored it.

'That,' Ma-Ma said when it was over, 'was an excellent movie.'

The next day, as Ma-Ma taught me how to make *sui-jai gou* – a steamed rice-flour pancake packed with artery-clogging cured meat – I turned on my laptop speakers so we could listen to the movie's soundtrack while we cooked. As Ma-Ma fried massive salmon heads in a pan, she began to sing along to the Chinese songs. I realised I'd never heard her sing in the whole time I'd known her. Hearing this eighty-something woman sing was bizarre and beautiful, like overhearing the mournful song of a mythological creature like a bunyip or a sasquatch.

Later that evening, I packed the car with my bags, humming the same odd Chinese tune my grandma had been singing. On the way out, I accidentally brushed my arm on her bush of *chow sie gau*, the dog-shit plant. I knew the stench would linger on me for the rest of the night. As I started the engine and watched her disappear in my rear-view mirror, I realised I'd enjoyed myself at the Gardens. Nothing about the place had depressed me at all. There were no sad people, no sad smells. As I drove past the other retirement homes, glimpsing the people inside going about their evenings, I realised the only thing that stank about the place was me, this guy with a weird smell on his fingers, reeking of youth.

So, You Are a Homo

∿ Maths

Despite being Asian, you have never been good at maths. In fact, no one in your family is good at maths, which is weird considering there are seven of you. But at night, lying in bed, you start doing sums in your head that keep you awake. These are terrible sums, unhealthy equations, and are designed to calculate the odds of you dying alone – which is something, you feel, more twelve-year-olds should think about seriously.

It starts like this. If one in ten people is homosexual – like you've been reading in the *Encyclopaedia Britannica*'s 'H' volume – that means that when you grow up, you'll have 10 per cent of the entire world's population as potential romantic candidates. Because there are roughly 6.7 billion people in the world, this equates to 670 million people at your disposal. That's a lot of people, you figure.

However, half of those 670 million people will be female: gay women who are more colloquially known as 'lesbians' (also according to the *Encyclopaedia Britannica*). That cuts the number in half. You now have 335 million homosexual men in the world. At this stage, 335 million still seems like a giant number, a number that remains on the comforting, ginormous, impossible-to-comprehend scale. 335 million is excellent; the odds that you won't die alone are favourable.

Still, you neither want to be a pederast nor the victim of paedophilia. Factoring in age of consent laws and boundaries of good taste, you narrow your pool to homosexuals from the ages of eighteen to, say, a generous thirty-five. Now, if average life expectancy around the world is roughly sixty-five years – and you get this figure by looking up the CD-ROM version of *Encarta* – your preferred age range accounts for only a quarter of the world's population. You're now left with 83.75 million people who may want to love you, and whom you may want to love back.

But the 'love you / love you back' part of the equation is where this mathematical formula becomes more complicated, and begs the question: *Who do you find attractive?* This is difficult for a twelve-year-old boy to know. But judging by your school-yard crushes so far, those people would include your friend Gerry, who has the most sculpted, handsome face you've ever seen on a prepubescent; and David, who already has visible and bulging pectoral muscles, though he is only six months into puberty. You also realise there are traits in boys you definitely *don't* find attractive. For instance, you cannot stand long nails. Hair cannot have dandruff, even though you are prone to this condition yourself, especially in winter when the air becomes dry, making your scalp itchy and flakey.

What else? Deformities. You're reminded of a boy in your gymnastics class, Martin, who had a condition whereby his big toe was fused to his second toe, which basically made it one giant toe with two toenails attached, and you clearly remember the moment during floor stretches when you realised that Martin would never be able to wear thongs on the beach, and you began to dry-retch. Which is a shame, really, because everything else about Martin you found quite physically appealing. Still, fused-together toes will need to be ruled out.

You start thinking about other physical deformities – not just fusion of the toes, but gigantism of the face, or dwarfism of the hands, and realise you won't be able to handle any of this. Disabilities may be okay, though. If they are deaf, that will be fine. Your cousin is deaf, and she lip-reads and talks, and has taught you some sign language, which you think is quite a sophisticated and *performative* language. In fact, maybe you'd even *prefer* a deaf guy as a partner. You surprise yourself by thinking mental disabilities might be okay too, but it would depend on the severity, of course. If disability were ranked on a scale of one to ten, one being the mildest, maybe a 'three' would be acceptable as a potential partner. Especially if they were handsome. Would you go out with a blind person, though? It's difficult to know.

Goddammit, you are one *choosy* faggot, aren't you? And what's with the arrogance? Hell, it might even be preferable that they be blind, because right now you are developing terrible acne, a violent rash on your face that is becoming so invasive you're not sure it'll ever completely disappear. Having a partner with poor vision might help your chances: if they can't see you, you feel confident you could win them over with witty banter.

It's hard to keep up with the maths by this stage. You're pretty confused. But let's say you find a fifteenth of all the world's available homosexuals attractive, and that a fraction of those – say, a twenty-fifth (this is generous, you know) – will find you attractive in return. That's about 2.23 million homosexuals left. But realistically, there will only be so many countries you'll be able to visit in your life, and only so many places you can be at

once. It would be impossible to encounter all of these homosexuals in your lifetime. Divide them by an arbitrary number
– say sixty-seven.

In the end, that leaves 33,283 people. And although that
seems like a lot, you are also lazy. Those 33,283 people could be
anywhere: Nepal or Idaho, Stockholm or Bosnia. Where would
you find the time and money to meet these people and make
them your boyfriends?

By this stage, it becomes clear that you'll die alone, after all.
Oh, it's sad, isn't it? Coming to the end of this equation makes
you weep into your BMX pillow – but you cry softly and silently,
because your brother, with whom you share a room, might
wake up and tell you to shut the hell up. But weep you must,
because it's unhealthy to keep those feelings in and it feels
good to cry, doesn't it? No one understands you; no one will
ever understand the pain you feel. Jesus Christ, you must be the
saddest person in the world right now, and you begin to pray that
it's somehow possible to train yourself to become heterosexual.
Perhaps you will write a song about how sad you are. Perhaps
you will write some poetry, start a journal. Maybe you will
compose a mournful song with your plastic Yamaha clarinet,
even though all you can play right now are major scales and
'Watermelon Man.'

As you shed tears onto your pillow, you realise that you're
actually quite enjoying this, and that it's the sort of thing that
might win you an Oscar some day. You get out of bed, tears fresh
on your face, race to the bathroom and close the door. You turn
on the lights and examine your tear-streaked face. If you can
summon tears on cue, you might make something of yourself as
an actor after all. With the right lighting, these tears streaming

down your cheeks might look cinematic. If only you could do something about that acne, though. It really does look fucking awful.

∽ COMMUNITY

Years later, when you leave home for the first time, you become really, really gay. You get an eyebrow ring; you start ordering pornography on VHS; you borrow gay-themed books from the library and attend rock concerts where the drummer or bassist is a lesbian, and this feels edgy at the time. Because you recently won a gold pass to an independent cinema chain and are entitled to free movies for a year, you've now seen the movie *Jesus' Son* five times solely in order to stare at Billy Crudup's face. You watch the gay British coming-of-age drama *Get Real* over and over again, even though one of your friends said she found it 'overly earnest.' This offends you a little, because at this stage of your life, you're nothing *but* earnest. Gay jokes aren't funny anymore. The suppression of the lesbian-gay-bisexual-trans-gender-and-intersex community is *real*. Everything is serious, and the stakes are high. This is not a drill; this is really *happening*.

At university, one of your writing assignments asks you to profile a person or organisation from a minority community. As a newly minted homosexual yourself, you decide to profile the country's longest-running LGBTI radio program, which happens to be located in your home town. All that history right on your doorstep. You take this as some sort of sign.

The community radio station broadcasts from a small hub around the corner from an adult shop that sells vibrators and assless leather chaps. You had expected people in punk T-shirts and mohawks, but the radio volunteers more or less look and smell like you: ripped-up cargo pants; piercings in their face; lack of deodorant. Peeling concert posters are papier-machéd onto the walls, and stuffing pokes out from the sofas. This all strikes you as very authentic; very real.

You talk to some of the volunteers. The place, you discover, is full of political dissenters, and has a long history of resistance and socialist protest. This station has been the headquarters of 'some fucked-up shit,' they tell you. However, someone adds dryly, the thing about anarchists and socialists is that they think changing the toilet paper is *bourgeois* – and this is why, on some days, the place smells like an open sewer. No one laughs at this, so you aren't sure whether it is a joke. But she is right: the place sort of stinks, at least tonight.

The three men who run the radio program are friendly, and you watch them present the show from a seat in the studio, which for some reason smells of eggs. Even though they are at least ten, twenty, maybe thirty years older, you feel as though you've finally found *your people*. On the show, they talk about upcoming LGBTI events, read out accommodation notices and play an interview with a local bisexual man who makes pop music in his suburban bedroom. The music is awful, pretty much unlistenable, but you don't say anything because you don't want to be mean-spirited.

Afterwards, you all have coffee together so you can interview them for your assignment. During the interview, one of them tells you that closeted men and women from all over the state have written to him, saying that they regularly drive for kilometres to the outskirts of their local shire, just so they can pick up the station's signal and listen in. *If I didn't have your show*, they write to him, *I would have committed suicide by now.*

This strikes you as heartbreakingly sad: people driving in their cars at night to the middle of nowhere, killing the engine and listening, alone in the dark.

The radio presenters tell you about all the hardships queer people suffer in your state, such as how the age of consent laws render you a criminal in your own home. When they ask for your age and you tell them you're seventeen, everyone leans in conspiratorially. 'So, did you know,' they ask, 'that you wouldn't be able to have anal sex ... *right now*?' *What?*, you think, *You mean here?* No, you did not know that, you say. After you finish the interview, they say they're impressed by your journalistic skills. The presenter tells you they need volunteers – *young* volunteers, especially – who can speak to the city's queer youth. It would only be one evening a fortnight. And because you are interested in the 'community' and all the hardships you face together, you accept and say *yes*.

Everything on the show must be gay. You find this out quickly. The music you play must be gay, even though at this stage, you only know about Morrissey, Elton John, k.d. lang and Rufus Wainwright. You do not want to play Melissa Etheridge. Once, after you play a P.J. Harvey song, the announcer asks you on air what P.J. Harvey has to do with the gay community and you can't muster a response. 'She's gay-friendly?' you mumble. Even if someone or something isn't gay, this announcer will *make* it gay. Once, while interviewing Elliott Smith, one of your favourite singers, he asked Smith how his sexuality had influenced his music career. 'Dude,' Smith eventually replied, 'I'm *not* gay.'

You are not good at panelling the show, and you sometimes leave dead air because you are nervous and freak out. At one point, the presenter intervenes and, in a flash of irritation, calls you 'unprofessional' on air, which is sort of humiliating. He is a very earnest and serious man sometimes. The relationship becomes tense. One night, when you and another young presenter share a glib, good-natured joke about anal sex, he cuts in and says without warning, 'And of course, we all know it's very important to evacuate one's *bowels* before engaging in anal sex.' There is silence for at least five seconds, which is a very long time on radio. As you cut to a song you realise right there, at the age of seventeen, your community spirit has died, before it even had a chance to develop.

∾ LOSING IT

As soon as you turn eighteen, you rally a bunch of friends and head directly to the Beat, the city's largest gay nightclub. In the past few weeks, the place has lost the 'B' from its flashing neon sign, so passers-by simply see the word 'EAT,' which everyone jokes is far more appropriate. The club has been described to you as everything from a 'meat market' to 'a goddamned cock buffet,' which makes you slightly ill, since you've never really liked buffets – all that food. Your friend Romy later tells you that after leaving this club one night, she found a slug of semen inexplicably on her shoulder.

Upon entering, you hit the Cockatoo Club bar (you'll only understand the play on words years later: 'cock or two') with the sole intention of getting devastatingly drunk. You drink everything in sight: vodka, beer, wine, champagne. This is dangerous, because alcohol acts quickly on your 48-kilogram frame. You examine yourself in various mirrors throughout the evening. What you are wearing looks good to you, but is actually a jumbled mess: brown beads; a shirt with an obnoxious play on the

Nike logo; orthodontic braces stained bright yellow by eating Indian food; suede pointed shoes that make you look like an elf. You will remember this outfit in years to come, wondering what you were thinking.

Nevertheless, you are shameless. You spend the entire evening fawning over a guy in the corner who has an ironic haircut and is dressed in army disposals. He looks heterosexual, and maybe this is a part of the appeal; part of the danger. Staring at him, you are already having conversations with him in your head; although you've never spoken to him, you already find him witty and intelligent, and begin to laugh out loud, rehearsing the moment when the two of you are actually talking. This is how drunk you are.

You're about to say hello when someone taps you on the shoulder and asks if he can buy you a drink. You haven't seen this guy before, but already you think he is fetching. He is basically the same height and frame as you, but he has very straight teeth. After chatting for a while, he tells you that you're the most attractive man he's seen in ages, and it's the first time anyone's ever said anything remotely like that. You didn't even know it was possible that anyone could think of you that way.

When you are so drunk you can barely see, you insist that he takes you to his place. He is quite sober; you are quite drunk. Despite his protests that he's just come out of a long-term relationship and wants to 'take it slow,' you drag him out of the club with force. You surprise even yourself at the strength you've suddenly developed.

At his place, you proceed to sprawl on his futon, unflinchingly nude. When you are both finally naked and making out, his flatmates come home and tap on the bedroom windows.

'Better be wearing a condom, you two!' You don't remember much, except that at one point he grimaces and says you have beer breath. After that, you pass out.

The next morning, you wake up with a head like an anvil and breath like a bin. But you look over at this stranger and think you've done quite well, considering. You've also had your best sleep in years; the futon is supportive, and it's the first bed you've ever slept in that isn't a single-frame mattress. You make a mental note to buy something similar if you ever have enough money, because the share-house bed you're sleeping in is destroying your back. Walking home from this guy's place, feeling crusty and smelling like a homeless person, you suddenly feel like a new man.

∽ THE ONE

In the end, you don't have to look too hard to find a proper boyfriend. In fact, in keeping with your laziness, you've already met him: you went to high school together. He was in the year below you: you played the clarinet; he sang in the barbershop quartet. You were both awkward-limbed boys, one with bad acne and an orthodontic plate (you), and the other with a pigeon-toed posture and the face of a choirboy (him).

You first became friends during a high-school music tour to the United States. With a group of about forty students and staff, you toured America's Bible Belt, wearing a specially designed uniform consisting of a polka-dot vest with a crucifix embroidered on the breast – a garment so awful and non-gender-specific that it immediately transformed you into a travelling troupe of Christian hermaphrodites. With the band, you played 'Come in from the Rain' in the Caucasian suburbs of

Los Angeles, and the theme song from *Jag* in San Diego sports stadiums. With the vocal quartet, he sang 'And So It Goes' in a demountable Christian school in Phoenix, a place where the students had names like Timofee – one F, two Es – the girls weren't allowed to wear trousers, and everyone prayed for the souls of aborted foetuses. His host family constantly asked him if he was 'a fag.'

When his quartet performed Billy Joel's 'The Longest Time,' you eyed him off, thinking his nervous bumbling was sort of adorable. Although it was the era of grunge, he was comically clean-cut, like a young blond prince from a Disney cartoon musical. But his innocent features belied a misanthropic streak. When told he would be spending the day at Disneyland, he became nauseous and refused to participate. When forced, he kicked the rubbish bins in protest and picked flowers from the Disneyland gardens, only for a gigantic butch female security guard to ask him what the *hell* he thought he was doing. His behaviour was borderline autistic, you admitted, but there was something about this boy, mouthing off and swearing in the happiest place on earth, that appealed to you.

Years later, you work alongside each other at your father's restaurant. You're on university holidays and he has just finished high school. Several things have changed, the most obvious being his hair, which has exploded into a wild blond mess. Gone are the short back and sides; now it covers his eyes and curls up in plumes around his head, a white man's afro. He also has stubble now, which strikes you as dangerous, and you have a sudden urge to see him naked.

It is New Year's Eve at the restaurant and the two of you work your way through a line of takeaway customers so long that it stretches down the street, its members drunk and hurling abuse at each other and the staff. The countdown to the new year is joyless, since everyone is so busy they could collapse. When you both leave, it's way past 1 a.m., so you buy alcohol and wander off together. You run into your older sister, Candy, and take turns giving her drunken piggybacks through the streets. When she finds her friends, the two of you walk together, taking swigs of cheap fizzy crap from the bottle, pushing each other around in shopping trolleys you find in empty carparks. Eventually, inebriated and suggestible, you start messing around in the sand dunes as the sun rises, while elderly couples walk past on their early morning New Year's strolls. You're pretty sure they see everything.

In the following days, he denies he is gay – it's all very dramatic. But one evening, at a party you attend together, the two of you leave discreetly, without any words, and start smashing your faces into each other with such violence that his five o'clock shadow eventually rips off the outer dermis of your skin. You roll over ants' nests until you're covered in welts. Finally, when you take a break, you realise you have somehow rolled down a hill and ended up in the carpark of a private hospital. With dirt all over your bodies and clothes, you hold hands and ask, *Where the hell are we?*

Time passes; hair changes. There's his blond afro to begin with, followed by his brown military mutton-chops. Next up is the prison-issue shave, which evolves into corporate back-and-sides and then rockabilly man-child. You're together, you break up, you're together, you live together. Nicknames change over the years, but the one that never changes is *monkey*, because of the way he holds on to you like a baby orangutan in his sleep.

Sleeping at night, you think about the people who spend their lives alone, and you wonder how people can possibly bear it. As you lie in bed together, you realise people all over the country are driving out to the outskirts of their towns, just to hear the faintest signal that there are other people like them in the world.

It's unlikely that the two of you ended up together. When people ask how long you've been together, the answer sounds like a long time. Other couples – including your parents – have gotten married and bred children in far less time. Sometimes, the figures scare you. But one night, you get out of bed and do the sums – this time with a calculator – and discover that the chance you found each other at all is exactly 0.0049 out of 100. You even have to adjust some of the decimal points in your calculator to work out the maths, because the sum is so extreme, so beyond conceivable limits, that the calculator originally gives you an error message.

Wrecking Ball

Spend enough of your childhood in any one house and you'll end up dreaming about it for the rest of your life. I've spent a decade living in other places – an apartment with my boyfriend, a sprawling Queenslander with flatmates, a Cambodian hostel where I was almost hospitalised for dysentery – but I've only dreamed about those places once or twice. Everything comes back to my childhood home. Sometimes, the house will have morphed in my dreams: my sisters' bedroom will be plagued with gremlins, or there'll be a secret annexe in the study and a rollercoaster in the living room. But it's essentially the same place. The same narrow hallway; the same boxy bedroom. Even though I spent my entire teen years wanting to get the hell away from there, my subconscious keeps surprising me by announcing it never wanted to leave. Go figure.

*

In most ways, the house is pretty unremarkable. A three-bedroom thing built in the late '70s, it was constructed with bricks the colour of dried shit and windows covered in security screens and fly-mesh: a practical choice, but not what you'd call pretty. Even when it was brand-new, I couldn't imagine potential buyers in the garage scanning the prospectus, looking over the place and thinking, *Wow*.

Being perched next to one of the busiest intersections on the Sunshine Coast made the place convenient, though not exactly private. The road outside my house linked the region's towns and motorways, and we had constant traffic beyond our fence. While most people might look over their backyard fence to see a council park or next-door neighbours, we saw Linfox trucks and thick black diesel exhaust. For seventeen years, I fell asleep to the sound of vans changing gears and the constant clicking of pedestrian-crossing buttons.

Before the local council improved the traffic lights, we were the ones who called ambulances when car accidents happened. We'd be watching TV or reading magazines when, out of nowhere, we'd hear the high-pitched wail of skidding tyres before bracing ourselves—

'*Whoa.*'

—for the smashing of metal and glass. It was always so loud; it felt like it was happening in our living room. Without saying a thing, we'd bolt outside, peer over the fence and scan the shattered windscreens and car bodies, all smashed up like they were made of aluminium foil. If the drivers were upright, out of their cars and screaming at each other, we'd call the police. If we saw blood on the road, we called triple zero.

Some nights, drunken men would vomit or piss outside our fence, or throw beer bottles into the yard that we'd pick up the next morning. Other times, sad-looking men in their forties and fifties – hammered with alcohol, freshly kicked out of their homes – would loiter in our garden like it was a public park. They were the worst. We'd be playing Monopoly or Upwords when one of us would see a grotesque face at the window, peering in like an apparition, and we'd all start to scream.

'Get down!' Mum once hissed at us. 'Get down and turn off the lights!'

The kids raced around the house, switching off lights until our entire house was plunged into darkness. This way, we could see out into the streets, but no one could see inside. As we moved silently from room to room, we picked up makeshift weapons along the way – tennis racquets, frying pans, a spiked netball pump – and tracked the stranger's movements. A security light traced him to a spot outside the bedroom I shared with Andrew. The five kids huddled behind a bed frame, watching him all lit up.

'Do you reckon he's a robber?' I whispered.

'Well, Mum's calling the police,' Andrew whispered back. 'Either way, he shouldn't be there.'

'You should scream at him,' Candy said. Michelle and Tammy huddled into her, close to tears. 'You should go out there with a *knife*. Chop off his dick.'

'What if *he* has a knife, dickhead?'

Tammy sucked her thumb, watching the exchange.

'You know karate,' I said to Andrew.

The stranger peered into the window and we all ducked. When he turned away again, swaying slightly, Candy whispered sharply.

'Both of you, shut *up*,' she said. 'He can hear you. And I don't think Mum wants *anyone* chopping anybody up.'

Mum came into the room with a small torch in one hand and a kitchen cleaver in the other. 'I've called the police,' she whispered. 'And if that man comes anywhere near us, I'll cut off his balls.'

The police never came, not then or the dozen other times it happened. The drunks were probably harmless, but we had reason to be paranoid. By the mid-'90s, the Sunshine Coast had become a hub for One Nation supporters. More than once, family friends of ours were found bruised and bashed, after late-night encounters with violent men in petrol stations. Passing drivers would occasionally scream at us as we climbed into the van in our school uniforms in the morning, or as we crossed the road to get groceries in the afternoon.

'Go *home*!' they hollered. And as the traffic lights turned green, they'd rev their engines, blast their horns and give us the finger before laughing like jackals, speeding off in a fumy cloud of black. Sometimes they threw stuff at us: apple cores, beer cans and burger wrappers. At first, this new experience was disorientating. What kind of person screams at a child in knee-high socks, holding a clarinet case? What had we ever done to them? It seemed so unfair.

'No respect,' my mother said, watching them drive away in utes. 'People have *no respect*.'

There was something so powerless about standing still while your tormentors got to drive away. It felt as though they got away with it, while you were left behind to shake your pathetic little fist in their dust. When stuff like this happened, I'd fantasise about owning guns or grenades, or make elaborate plans to fill water-bombs with rotten milk and shit. Eventually, we started giving the finger back, my mother included: a bunch of school-aged kids in private-school uniform and their tiny Asian mother, all flipping the bird. It might have been badly ventilated and packed full with clutter; it might have been roach-infested and a hive of domestic tension; but it was our home, and we weren't going anywhere.

*

Years later, when all the kids had moved out, my mother found herself living by herself in the house. The abuse from strangers had stopped, but the trash and beer bottles continued. By this stage, the house was falling apart. After thirty years, it was as though it had aged in dog years and was now on its last legs. Door-knobs had fallen off wardrobes. Kitchen cabinets sat at weird angles, leaning downwards to the stovetop like a pair of angry eyebrows. Light fittings had disappeared and rooms were now lit by naked bulbs. Our wooden cubby house had rotted away like an abandoned fort, its giant rusted nails exposed to the rain.

On one of those rainy days, I visited Mum and started talking about her future, now that she no longer had to take care of us. I thought it would make for a happy, optimistic conversation, a forward-looking plan of adventure for a gung-ho empty-nester.

'So, what do you think, Mum?' I asked brightly. 'What's the plan?'

Mum looked at the wall blankly.

'I will die in this house,' she said. 'I will die here alone.'

There was an uncomfortable pause between us.

'Right-o,' I said.

When I got back to the city, deflated and depressed, my boy-friend suggested she sell the house and move away from the coast. 'If she sold the land and moved to the city, she'd have a better house as well as savings. Not only would she be in a better place, she wouldn't have to rely on your dad or the pension.' Scott had always been the one who could see my family from the outside, the one who came up with ideas when everyone else had run dry. 'Your mum would be so much happier if she moved to the city,' he said. 'And so would you. Everything she loves is here.'

After setting up a house and land valuation, we found she was sitting on prime real estate. Mum was thrilled.

'Yes!' she said to Scott and me breathlessly. '*Yes!* Why didn't I think of this before? It will be like my second divorce. I'll *divorce* this house like I *divorced* your father. Yes, I will drive the bulldozer myself! So many bad memories in this house. We should just knock it *down*.'

When I called the other siblings, everyone was supportive, but I could also hear something else in their voices, a tinge of heartbreak. Michelle had only moved out a year earlier and still referred to the place as home.

'Would they really knock it down?' she asked. 'Would we watch?'

That night, thinking about Michelle's question, I surprised myself by starting to cry.

'Benjamin?' Scott said, turning over. 'What's wrong?'

I didn't know what to say. It was hard to articulate what I felt. As much as I hated that house, I think I felt sorry for it too.

*

Someone I know is having his house demolished soon, and I've asked to come along and watch. I'm curious to see how it all works. What sort of equipment do you need to tear down someone's house? How long does it take? Can the family who owned the house contribute to its destruction? Can they bring sledgehammers and drive the bulldozers, or does this represent an occupational health and safety violation? And what happens to the rubble afterwards? Where do the remains of a house get buried?

My childhood home might be bog-standard brick, but I'd

like to think that standing there for thirty years has fortified it to the point where it will need dynamite and wrecking balls to break it down, some heavy-duty arsenal. But I know it doesn't take much to make a house like that disappear. I've watched houses being torn down on the internet, and usually all that's needed is a single bulldozer, while the former residents whoop and cheer in the background, getting high on watching their home be obliterated. It looks like fun.

In my mind, I can already see what will happen leading up to the demolition of our house. Tammy, the photographer, will document the entire process, from the signing of the papers to the boxing-up of childhood artefacts for storage. She'll be the one who'll zoom in close to archive the childhood vandalism left on the walls, the stuff we scrawled as kids that we'll never see again. Michelle, a writer, will pen some tragi-comedy about it, something heartbreaking and absurd. Candy and Andrew, the practical, sensible ones, will look over the paperwork and make sure things are in order. And when we've finally kissed the house goodbye, offering it our thousand quiet apologies, we'll take turns recording the carnage on video: trees being uprooted, our termite-infested cubby house being smashed into the ground, the graveyards of long-dead mice, guinea pigs and goldfish exposed by the bulldozer, before its giant metal claw tears down the walls, smashing it all into the dirt.

Or maybe we won't be there at all. Perhaps we'll be as far away as possible, pretending there's nothing to see. I can picture my family in the city, at my mother's new place, 100 kilometres away from ground zero. By that stage, she'll be pouring champagne as we unwrap her furniture, willing ourselves to forget that the other place existed at all.

Whatever happens, we'll eventually have to drive past our old place. To visit my boyfriend's mother, my cousins or my dad, we'll need to take the main road where the house once stood. It will be disorienting to see it gone, and I'll probably pull a right at the traffic lights out of habit. Who knows what will have replaced our house by then? Maybe there'll be shops or a block of apartments, a government office or a real-estate agent, or maybe a combination of those things stacked one on top of the other. People who've driven past the house for decades will struggle to remember what once stood there, the same way you struggle to remember old businesses once they've been replaced by shiny new shopfronts. *There was this Asian family who used to live there*, they'll think. *A whole bunch of kids. Four? Five? Six? I can't remember. And their weird mother: this funny Chinese woman who referred to herself in the third person and let the grass grow long.* Really, it would be so easy to forget anyone ever lived there at all. In the end, the house could be something I only imagined or dreamed about, something only a select few of us remember, or just something I made up for a story.

Acknowledgements

Even though this book is dedicated to them, it would be insane not to thank my family properly. So Mum, Dad, Candy, Andrew, Tammy and Michelle: thank you – not only for providing the source material, but also for letting me get away with this. You are my favourite people. I am proud to share your genetics, as well as your medical disorders.

I'm grateful to everyone at Black Inc. Chris Feik, my publisher and editor, is a prince. For his foresight (he knew this was a book before I did), patience, good humour and exceptional brain, I am completely indebted. Thanks to Sophy Williams, Denise O'Dea for her eagle eyes, Andrew Joyner for his exceptional illustrations, Thomas Deverall for his smart design and Nina Kenwood for championing me. Special thanks also to my agent and co-conspirator Benython Oldfield.

Many thanks to my various editors over the years, for encouraging me to write: Louise Bannister, Jo Walker and Lara Burke (*frankie*); Ben Naparstek (the *Monthly*); Sally Warhaft (formerly of the *Monthly*); Christine Middap, Karen Milliner and Cathy Osmond (*Qweekend*); Alan Attwood and co. (the *Big Issue*); Alison Boleyn and Michelle Hurley (*Sunday Life*); Rick Bannister (formerly of *Transit*), Ronnie Scott (*The Lifted Brow*); Kellie Chandler and Tom Doig (formerly of *Voiceworks*); Pat Whyte (formerly of *Scene*); and Rosemary Sorensen (formerly of the *Courier-Mail*). Thank you also to David Marr and Robyn Davidson for including two of these stories in their volumes of *The Best Australian Essays*.

Over the course of writing this book, Caro Cooper, Matthew Condon, Stuart Glover, Ben Green, Chloe Hooper, Bethany Jones and Alice Pung all answered odd questions, and I am much obliged. I have also been supported by the QUT Creative Writing department, Fiona Stager and the staff at Avid Reader bookstore and café, and the National Young Writers' Festival.

Thanks to my writing buddies – Romy, Rhianna, Christopher, Chris, Fiona, Daniel, Rowena, Dion, Anthony, Kris, Kirsten, Belinda, Cory, Mia, Kári and Sam, to name but a few – and especially Michaela McGuire, Krissy Kneen, Alice Pung (again) and Marieke Hardy for being the book's first readers. Extra thanks to Lorelei Vashti for late-night conversations, and to my glorious wife Anna Krien (another first reader), without whom, I would have gone insane. To all my non-writerly friends between Brisbane and Melbourne: thank you too. My mother's right. I *am* lucky.

Thank you to Val Spark, for the food and support, and to Ken Spark, whom we all miss. And finally, thank you to Scott Spark – my smart, criminally handsome, funny-as-a-bastard boyfriend – whom I not only adore, but who makes all things, including this book, possible.